LOVE IS SOMETHING YOU DO

FREDERICK B. SPEAKMAN

LOVE IS SOMETHING YOU DO

FLEMING H. REVELL COMPANY

"Somebody Up There Likes Me," lyric by Sammy Cahn,
music by Bronislau Kaper. Copyright 1956 Loew's Inc.
Rights throughout the world controlled by Leo Feist Inc.,
New York, N.Y. Used by permission.

To Zoe

CONTENTS

CONTENTS

LOVE IS SOMETHING YOU DO

"Fondness, affection for people can be cultivated, but it cannot at will be turned on or off
like a faucet. Christian love must be something
other than that. I'm fairly certain . . . that if I'm
required to love . . . it must be as a principle,
not as an emotion."

—*One of the Sisters*

1

LOVE IS SOMETHING YOU DO

It was at their house on High Street that I first learned to be suspicious of the word "quaint." That is what people who didn't know them well called these sisters, these by now elderly maiden ladies: "quaint." But there were those of us who would have shifted the consonants. We learned to call them "saints," though I know they'd have been as annoyed at that title as they'd have been amused at the other.

Different they certainly were. They dressed for warmth and comfort instead of appearance whenever they went out in New Jersey winters, which was often enough to keep their chauffeur in a constant state of shock. I'll not soon forget the effect of the elder sister swathed in what I can only describe as a white fox rug, from neck to high-booted ankles, and a matching Cossack cap, plunging through knee-deep snow as if it weren't there, moving faster at her age than I've ever moved, to deliver jellies to some indisposed friend or to catch up on her personal and extensive list of shut-ins.

They had built their huge, pleasant house in a section of town that was by now a jumble of austerely modern homes and 1920

11

nondescript, and what someone unkindly has called William-Jennings-Bryan-Spanish. But their house defied classification for it was their own plan. There had been a towering tree on the property that they couldn't bear to let go, so they built their house around it. The thick trunk went right up through the center of the three floors, comfortably encased by its own tailor-made walls, the top of it spreading out over the many levels of the roof like a giant edition of one of the sisters' own perky parasols. I'm sure that sounds silly, but it wasn't. Nothing they did was silly.

Inside their home was a furnished blend of the old and real with the new and gay that had to be sampled to be believed. A canary named Billy—yes, "Billy"—would be out of his cage, chances were, flying from room to room and chair-back to lamp, fluttering and chirping like the sisters themselves. "Billy's out for his constitutional," they'd airily explain, and Billy must have built himself quite a constitution, for you'd rarely catch him in his cage! The dour Scotch maid would be dusting indefatigably in the dining room, a maneuver that always struck me as strictly make-believe. For I was certain that dust, by virtue of the incessant warfare waged against it, had long since forsaken this house. The younger sister would apologize for the clutter of books and papers on or about her desk, for she would be writing a paper to give at a woman's club on some astonishing theme, a critique of some book not available in English, or an analysis of recent Soviet foreign policy. The grand piano—no baby grand, mind you—would be piled high with an assortment of outgoing parcel post that would have done credit to a village post office, addressed to every exotic port-of-call on the map. I'd like to know how many missionaries' wives they'd never met received from them, in a given year, some sage and practical remembrance, or what was surely even better for morale, some gift bright and useless and enjoyable. The elder sister, if not on the run somewhere, might well be perched on the love seat near the fire, a corner of the afghan across her shoulders and knitting socks with an intensity that suggested every child in Asia might well go barefoot next winter except for her constant output!

It was all as Mid-Victorian as your great uncle Albert—yet as contemporary as this morning's paper—and as wise as Walter Lippmann, and as sharp as a Yankee trader, and at the same time as kind as womankind alone can be, and as Christian as a page from the New Testament. For occasionally, you know, what looks decent *is* decent. Occasionally, and this always fools the cynic, things are what they seem. This seemed good, and it was.

It was good, I know, for a fledgling clergyman who was just beginning to be caught in the pull between what a Christian church should be and what it usually is. I was just awakening really to the wide obvious gulf between what we as modern ministers should accomplish, and the ragged little fraction of that which our all too human limitations will allow us to accomplish. And what a refuge this home was, where one particular easy chair was called "my chair." And there would be a Bible usually opened to the Book of Job or to Isaiah, for these were their favorites, and from these they preferred me to read, just as their father had read to them before the fire.

It was there in "my chair" one cold winter afternoon with the log fire as high as my spirits were low, that the name of a certain man had been mentioned, a man who had meant trouble for all of us, for no reasons we could fathom; every fence we tried to mend seemed only to encourage him to be more difficult. I had exploded concerning this gentleman; then, conscience twinging, I had commented on my own explosion, "But there I go! There you have it! How in heaven's name, as Christians, are we supposed to love a man like that?"

The younger sister glanced up at me and removed her glasses and stroked her cheek with the temple-piece slowly in a way she had when she was measuring her words. "You sound as if you expected yourself to be able to be fond of him. But that's nonsense, isn't it? I don't believe Jesus Christ is interested in nonsense. Fondness, affection for people can be cultivated, but it cannot at will be turned on or off like a faucet. Christian love must be something other than that. I'm fairly certain Christ understands that *if I'm required to love that man, it must be as a principle, not as an emotion!*"

Do certain words and phrases come back to you, like certain songs or snatches of melody, bringing with them the very atmosphere in which you first heard them? I never rehearse those words without some sense of the house on High Street, and even the canary and the afghan and a cold wind whistling a wild tune outside, but inside a log fire that seemed uncommonly bright. I repeat them to myself often, for across ten years they've impressed me increasingly as a big step toward an operational answer to this embarrassing mandate of Christian love.

Deep in our hearts there isn't any thrust of the gospel that leaves us quite so uncomfortable. We know, all of us, how shabbily we treat it. "Behold, how these Christians love one another!" Yes, just do behold it. "By this shall all men know that ye are my disciples, if ye have love one to another." What a pulverizing indictment!

So often, we know that we don't even try. We may never have said it to ourselves in so many words, but most of us, somewhere along the road, have said something like this: "Love of all mankind is church talk which never comes to grips with people as they really are. My hat's off to anyone who can make any kind of go of it. But my heart is made—and remember I didn't make it—my heart came equipped with a certain stub-

born earthy stuff that simply can't go around emoting over
the many unloveworthy people I know, so there's no point in
pretending that I can. That crude lout down at the office who
so deliberately needles my nerves, or that smooth liar who
took me in so completely yesterday, or that crass, strutting big
wheel who barged into our neighborhood, that one-time friend
who took advantage of my trust so shamelessly, or that other
who has so deliberately tossed away the values of life to grasp
and cherish the sickening and destructive forces—by what
magic am I supposed to feel anything but resentment, distrust,
and a justified desire to have nothing to do with such as these?"
Isn't that about the way the monologue would go, if we'd let it
speak?

*But what if Christian love was never meant to begin in the
way we feel toward people?* What if Christian wisdom dismisses
as quite obvious the kindergarten fact that of course you and
I will always be fond of some people, and not at all fond of
others? What if Christ never expected you and me to sit around
trying to force, trying to manufacture affectionate feelings
toward people who consistently dig and rub us the wrong way?
Wouldn't that refocus the picture?

You see, there is no virtue in being naturally fond of someone,
any more than there is any sin in being not at all fond of
someone else. It's what we do about these feelings that results
in the sin or the virtue.

Any pagan can say, "I will do good to that man, because as
a matter of emotion I like him!" It takes a Christian who has
made steady use of his Christian resources to be able to say,
"As a matter of emotion I dislike that man, *but I will do good
to him because as a matter of Christian principle, I love him.*"

Bishop Stephen Bayne of Seattle has been described by *Time*
magazine as one of the few Americans who can make real
Christian theology as warm and immediate as politics and

baseball. I relished his raging recently at a routine dilemma that occurs in every pastor's study. He tells of a couple that is planning to be married; they drop into the study by appointment, and they're early this time. If the minister hasn't been taken in by every fad of the moment he knows what he should talk to them about. He knows he should not for one moment pose as an amateur geneticist, or a clerical-collar sexologist, or, what's even worse, the bluff and hearty Good Humor Man who's to be M.C. at the wedding. He ought to talk to them about Christian love.

But it's there that he's caught, the Bishop insists, for if he knows enough to know what he should be talking about, he knows enough to know they won't be listening. Not really. They're emotionally anaesthetized, for all practical purposes, else they're so fatigued by the carnival their family and friends have put them through that they're past the point of cerebration. Chances are it will be a good six months before they awaken to the fact that they're still more or less the same self-centered human beings they were before, and then can begin the slow, wonderful, difficult task of growing toward each other day by day, choice by choice.

But how tell them that, now? How get in back of their riot of feelings to persuade them now that, even in marriage, love is *not* primarily something you feel! *Love is something you do!*

It would make the marriage vow a farce to imagine it means any two mortals can stand before God and solemnly promise he and she will feel tender and loving toward each other every moment till death does them part! For emotions come and go, and tenderness has its highs and lows, but the heart of Christian marriage is that one is able to vow thus before God: "I will act toward this person in a way that I will act toward no one else from now on, no matter what the climate or the season of my feelings. This love will find its measure in me in the things I *do*."

Now I know what a sudden leap it is from that to the rest of the people in your life, to the way we're meant to deal with acquaintances, with the owners of those elbows we jostle daily, with all those whose paths we just happen to cross in this suddenly frightened world, or with those strangers so abristle with antagonisms. But life is of a piece, and if this is true at the core of it, this must also hold out at the fringe of it: *it is wonderful to feel a warmth and glow toward other people.* I'm certain if we had Christ at our hearts oftener, we'd feel that warmth toward far more people than we do. But isn't it the first step toward realistic Christian love to admit that while there are many toward whom we feel no such warmth, *yet our Christian marching orders are to treat them as if we do?*

It's perfectly amazing how often the fondness can follow the deed. It's amazing how often the world's formula, "I'm fond of that man, so I helped him," finds the Christian reversal, "I helped that man so now I'm fond of him!" But whether that happens or not, what Christ talked about the most is still measured by what we do about it. Have you ever noticed that in His unavoidably clear picture of the Judgment, the King does not say to those on His right hand, "I was hungry and you felt sorry for Me—I was naked and you felt the shame of it along with Me—I was imprisoned and the manacles on my wrists hurt you too—I was sick and you were so sympathetic with Me"? All that would have been wonderful, but it wasn't what added up. What added up was the hungry that were fed, the naked that were clothed, the sick and the imprisoned that were helped. What a realist this Christ is! "Do you love people?" He asks. Then—"No, no, don't bother to tell Me how you *feel* about them. *What are you doing about them?*"

"What's so bad about that song? . . . I tell you in today's welter of near despair you should be grateful for anything in the popular vein that reminds the average man of God in any form, and quit this splitting of hairs about issues that the average among us isn't going to care about, no matter how worked up you get."

—*The Close Friend*

2

NOBODY UP THERE "LIKES" YOU

HE HAD BEEN laughing at me, this friend of mine with whom I so enjoy chewing over most any topic, because he has a faith that seems never to need an apology, and an eversharp mind that seems never to need honing. When he's quiet you know he's listening, not dozing; but when he speaks you listen, because he has something to say. I've never heard his conversation puddle down to a recital of his latest illnesses or mere chiffer-chaffer about last night's television schedule. What's more, he doesn't let me get by with a thing just because I'm a clergyman. In fact, I've often suspected that his only real difficulty with religion is that he has known too many clergymen too well. That can be a roadblock in any pilgrim's progress!

This was not an evening for heated discussion, heaven knows. The day had been a brute, a scorcher. The sun had seemed to linger deliberately, maliciously, at sunset, making certain it left enough discomfort to last through the night and get a running start on heating up tomorrow, and only late had the cool breeze come there in the yard; even the locusts

19

seemed to hush their rowdiness a moment as a token of grati-
tude for it. We should have been quietly enjoying it too,
gasping at it like stranded bass, there under the cloudless night
sky that seemed so uncommonly crowded with stars.

But no—a neighbor's radio was turned up to a volume that
should be illegal, except for baseball games. A song was being
sung, a popular religious song of the moment. I had filled my
lungs with that rare cool breeze and had launched into a
tirade about that song; that's when my friend laughed at me,
and said with the bluntness only close friends should use,
"Now you do sound like a preacher, and the worst variety of
preacher at that. A *closed-shop preacher,* a cleric who is so
afraid someone outside your union will have something to say
about religion. What's so bad about that song? You really
should welcome it. It's far more tuneful than most of our
hymns. It's reverently done, and it's rather well sung, for its
kind. What if it isn't too exactly theologically sound? Do you
think you'll ever really persuade the man in the street to give
a hoot about that? *I tell you in today's welter of near despair
you should be grateful for anything in the popular vein that
reminds the average man of God in any form,* and quit this
splitting of hairs about issues that the average among us isn't
going to care about, no matter how worked up you get!"

I'd hate to tell you how late we went at it, misusing that
rare cool breeze in a thermal manner for which it was not
meant. For he had a point to make, several points that scored,
but not his main point! I was ready to hand him my stuffy
ecclesiastical head and plead guilty to every charge he had
made—but not to his main charge! There he had fired a dangerous blank. *In today's confusion, if we are Christians, we
dare not be grateful for just anything that reminds men of
God in any form.* Because it could well be the wrong form!
That's just one more way of saying that it will not save

America to return to religion if the religion it returns to is a false religion. It cannot save the world to rediscover a faith in God, if its rediscovered faith is in the kind of God who isn't there!

We can saw off one little corner of that vast problem with this little song, which won't be with us long, but the problem it's a part of will be with us from now on. Yes, it's a tuneful song, tunful enough that to my deep annoyance I catch myself humming it. And yes, it's rather well done for that sort of thing, especially by Mr. Perry Como, and heaven knows in a day that's enraptured by Elvis Presley, Perry Como by comparison is someone devoutly to be grateful for. But not this song, because it comes so close to saying something all-important and it misses, and by missing, it says something altogether different. Listen to its words:

Somebody up there likes me! Somebody up there cares.

*   *   *

Whatever betide me, He'll comfort and guide me,
And stand beside me, right or wrong.
As sure as He likes the stars and the earth and the gentle sea . . .

Does it sound simple and nice and cozy and easy and comforting? It's all of that, but to Christians, religiously, it isn't worth the breath it takes to quote it. Religiously that lyric is a full-page ad for the thin, soupy, watered-down sentimentalism which so many people both inside and outside the churches today vaguely believe is the Christian religion, but which is of little more use against the perplexities of the lives we're trying to live than some child's sand castles on the beach would be against some stormy surging high tide.

That's why we bother to carp at it, to dignify it by noticing it. That's why in the name of Christ, we dare say to such a misreading of Him as this, "No, this is not what we mean by

faith. *Nobody up there 'likes' you!* Not in the way that suggests.
Our claim is that *Somebody up there loves you.*" And don't
think for a moment that it's the same. Between the two claims
lies all the difference you can crowd in between mere comfortable nonsense and a living faith.

We'll hurry over one mood of this song, which is the mood
of so much of the popular disc-jockey or after-dinner speech
piety of the day. We'll skip over this business of being
chummy, if you please, buddy-buddy, palsy with the Almighty,
this mood which at its worst becomes a sidling up to God
with a playful poke in the ribs and a kind of fraternity-rush
pat on the back. A famous actress said to a reporter, "Oh, to
me God's marvelous; He's just a livin' doll!" Yes, I gasped
too! Let's simply say in passing that you can look around and
test that sort of thing by its results. In the long, loud human
story it's doubtful if any faith that has ever really done much of
anything for or with anyone has started with that. It's doubtful if a man can really and meaningfully face the question,
"Is Anyone up there? And if so, what's He like? And what
does He have to do with me down here?" unless he brings
to that question every ounce of wonder and reverence and
humility and awe with which his heart is furnished, unless he
brings to that question some awareness of how much is at
stake for him now and forever in the very name, God.

For when we talk about Somebody Up There, we're not only
talking about the Master Craftsman of the universe, the Source
of all that is in this whole awesome ferris wheel of power and
immensities, a wheel so delicately balanced that in our little
corner of it a goldfinch can perch on an azalea bush and eye
the children as they laugh and run across the lawns on their
way to school. We're dealing not only with that incredibly in-
genious Designer whose age-old purposes have just in passing
made possible such a structure as the human eye, such a marvel

as the human brain, so unlikely a miracle as childbirth, so
prodigal and anonymous an exhibit as a sunset, so unimagin-
able a thing as springtime, so improbable a harmony as a
symphony. But when we say "God" with a capital "G" we're
also talking about the Great Person, the Heart at the heart of
everything on whom our very breath depends, who holds
every hour of our selfish, fragmentary little lives in the palm
of His claim on our obedience and trust. Since if He's God at
all, if He's any kind of God at all, then the whole meaning
of our lives depends on Him. Whatever importance or permanence there can be to this mixed and troubled struggle we
have on our hands, this queer quicksilver thing we call living,
this dreaming and wanting and willing and doing, this thread-
ing the needle between a few right things and so many wrong
things, this playing host to passions and feelings that can
wrench us and turn us monstrous or can lift us to high achievement and ennobling loyalties, this fearing and hoping and trying and failing and never being quite certain whether the
shining hours really make up for the days that hurt—any
possible importance or permanence there can possibly be in
your being you or my being me is all wrapped up in God, and
depends absolutely on who He is and what He's really like.

For me to answer that, the most important question life will
ever ask me, by saying, "Well, I've a reassuring feeling there
is Somebody Up There and He 'sort of likes me' "—that means
I've not only missed the boat, it means I've missed Christ,
have missed the big things Christ said and did and was, because for God just to like me would either mean He's somewhat fond of me in a casual, indulgent kind of way, or it
would mean that He approves of me. And neither of those is
true. God is not indulgently fond of me, viewing my constant
failures to live the way I should as the inevitable mischievous-
ness of some two-legged pet of His who is slightly inclined to

naughtiness! He will not, as this ballad so neatly urges, "Whatever betide me, He'll comfort and guide me, and stand beside
me, right or wrong!" If that's what He were like, our Creed
might read, "I believe in the Grandfatherhood of God," or if
you please, "I believe in the Aunt Sallyhood of God," but it
couldn't read the way it does now.

There's so much about me that He doesn't like, of which He
so deeply disapproves: my bluffing and strutting, my self-cen-
teredness and self-deceptions, my stubborn choosing of the
worse when I know the better, my willingness to treat and
manipulate people like things, my refusal ever to require of
myself the conduct I demand of others, my casualness about
those I've hurt but my hot-house, spoon-fed resentments of
all who hurt me, my blithe assumption that I'm forgiven for
things I won't forgive in others, my quickness to whine, my
morbid enjoyment of fear, my proneness to despair and blame
Him—where would that list stop? For God, because He is
God, is the constant, sleepless, unrelenting Enemy of all that
is wrong in me. That's the bass note today's song of faith
seems unable to hear or unwilling to sing: the Power Up
There is the unrelenting Enemy of all that's wrong with you
and me.

Because—He loves you so! We're almost embarrassed to say
it or hear it with so naïve a simplicity and plainness even from
a Christian pulpit, aren't we? We'd rather put it some other
way. But there isn't any other way to say it. Even when we've
cheapened that word "love" the way we have with so many
weak and counterfeit uses, still, when we try any other words,
we find them a good many sizes too small to say this unsayable
thing that still must be said. *Somebody Up There Loves You.*
Not because you deserve it or have earned it. You don't deserve it and you never will earn it. But because you're His!
Of course He likes, enjoys "the stars, the earth and the gentle

sea." But that hasn't anything to do with the way He feels about you. Do you enjoy flowers, your lawn, your home, some hobby? But that isn't in the same universe with the feeling about your child, or anyone you've ever loved with every pulse-beat of your being!

And that's still our clearest clue, the nearest we can come. What you have felt there at your best is an echo, a hint, a tiny mortal dose of how He feels about you. Remember, it doesn't make life any easier to believe that; in fact, I'm convinced in some ways it makes life more of a struggle. It doesn't make our hurts any less, our losses any easier. It doesn't cut down on the number of times we'll look up from some broken dream to ask, "God in heaven, why?" But it's the only faith under heaven that can bind earth's inconsistencies and bitter reversals together into any bundle of livability. This Christ lived to tell, died to prove, and rose to conquer by: in back of everything that seems to deny it, your life is a love story between the Almighty and you. It's the story of a love that will put us through whatever disciplines it takes for Him or for us, if only we can learn somewhere along the road to value what He values, hope what He hopes, and will what He wills, since only then can we reach the happiness He has wanted us to know all along.

That's our song. That's our Christian song. Maybe you can't sing it, but you can march to it!

"I'm afraid of God. I've always known that somewhere along the line I've got to deal with Him, and I'm just postponing that as long as I can."

—*Gabe Jennings*

3

THE TROUBLE WITH LOVING GOD

"JESUS SAID UNTO him, Thou shalt love the Lord thy God with all thy heart, and with all thy soul, and with all thy mind. This is the first and great commandment." Could He really have meant that? Could He really have meant what He seems to be saying—that the most urgent, the most necessary, the indispensable thing for a man to do is to love God in the way he thinks, in what he feels, in what he is? *How on earth does a human being ever go about loving God?*

Reverence for God—we know something of what that means; we've felt that ourselves, from time to time. Oh, not as often as we should have, to be sure, for our minds stay smothered and lathered over by the froth of the world, our hearts are bathed, soaked, drenched, steamed in this steady bath of busyness which we complain about so and yet enjoy so, like some narcotic. Still, there are those off-beat moments when we feel the awesomeness of Him who is behind it all. There are strange hours when the great old prayer makes sense: "O God, here am I of so little power and mean estate, yet lifting up heart and voice to Thee before whom all created things are as a dust and a vapor!" There are such hours, yet at their best they are only occasional hours, and could you possibly, by any stretching or warping of the word call what we feel then loving God? Hardly!

We have puzzling moments that are first or second cousin to that hour—Studdert Kennedy describes as the turning point of his life the night he walked alone on a lonely moor beside the sea. Above him was the great dark cyclorama of the heavens, and the stars—those tireless million engines of infinity—and down here not a sound but the night wind and the boom of the waves against the cliff. He was as alone as a man could be, and yet he was acutely conscious of Someone, a vast mysterious Someone other than himself, moving out there in the dark and among the tiny lights of those other worlds above him. He felt so like calling out, "Who's there?" He thought of the battlefield in France where he lay alone between the trenches and saw a moving figure coming toward him in the darkness, and wondered, if he whispered, "Who goes there?"—would the answer be a bullet, or a friendly word, or only silence? You and I have known the times which allow us at least to understand what he felt along that moor looking up and out and listening to the boom of the surf and the sound of the wind in the heather. *But could you possibly call that kind of puzzled, half-frightened, half-yearning searching a matter of loving God?*

Or perhaps we'd do better putting the question to other people than ourselves, to actual people. We might ask Ellen Durkin. We might just find Ellen at the Metropolitan Museum in New York this very Sunday afternoon, because on Sundays she always has a compulsion to do something self-educating though she knows that's probably a reaction to her annoyance at Sunday as a day of rest. She's from a small town in Ohio, and like a million other American girls she is quite attractive;

thanks to that accident, she considered her potentialities un-limited, and she emotionally outgrew her family, her friends, the town, the local church, the local library. She could never quite forgive them all for being "smalltown." She was so eager to meet "real people," as she put it, to be exposed to "real culture." Today, she can't quite forgive New York for being just another town, only bigger and lonelier and filled with more people like herself with even far less chance of finding each other. And if you found Ellen this afternoon (in the modern section of course; she would much have preferred sitting in the Rembrandt gallery, but there was not a chance of meeting anyone worth meeting before a Rembrandt; only out-of-towners gawked at a Rembrandt), and if you could evade her defenses and ask, *"Ellen, do you love God?"* she would look pained for a moment, as if remembering youthful days when she thought she did. She would answer in the flat tones of the defeated, "No. I try to think about God as little as I possibly can, because when I do think about Him, I deeply resent Him!"

Or could you ask Gabe Jennings? Gabe's still a bachelor in his late thirties, a key salesman for a firm in a mid-western city. You'd enjoy his company for a while, though you'd soon wonder how anyone could manage to remain such a stock type; he seems stamped out by some twentieth-century biscuit cutter. His long suit is his go-getting geniality and his aston-ishingly reasonable facsimile to the well-groomed virility you associate with full-page color ads of luxury items in the better magazines. He keeps himself in excellent physical condition in spite of quite a lenient personal moral code. Gabe is a healthy animal, and he devotes his spare hours to enjoying, being and remaining a healthy animal, and trying to forget he was ever meant to be or ever will be anything else. But Gabe Jennings would surprise you if you could get through the

practiced pretensions of his studied boyishness long enough
to ask, "*Do you love God?*" He'd look frightened, as if you had
mentioned a subject his set had promised each other never
to talk about. "No," he would answer, if he answered honestly.
"I'm *afraid* of God. I've always known that somewhere along
the line I've got to deal with Him, and I'm just postponing
that as long as I can."

You could ask Bill Pierce, Professor William Case Pierce,
esteemed at a West Coast college both as a teacher of men and
as a man himself. Bill Pierce attends a local church quite faith-
fully though he does not belong, and rarely will you hear him
airing any of his personal religious views, yet if he knew you
were sincere in asking him, "*Do you love God?*" he would not
dodge the question. He would pocket his reading glasses and
rub the tips of two fingers over the bridge of his nose in the
way he does when he's carefully measuring his words, and he
would answer, "I'm afraid that question has no real meaning
to me. I do not believe that there is no God. Yet I cannot say
I have a belief or a faith. All that I have is a hope. I hope
that there is in all these masses and energies and light years
around us some Great Awareness—so great that in spite of my
unimportance that Consciousness is at least a little concerned
about me and what happens to me and all these others like
myself involved in the experiment humanity. That naked hope
is my religion, and as a scientist I've as much intelligent right
to it as anyone who denies it. But I doubt if you could decorate
that slim a creed with any love of God!"

Oh, yes, I've changed the names of those people, but I
think I've been fair to them. They haven't been chosen at
random or just to sketch vignettes. *Every one of those reactions
suggests some standard roadblock every one of us will ever
and again be running up against as we try to love God.* Ellen
Durkin's tight-lipped resentment of God because of the way

her life seems to be turning out: you and I have a dose of that too, because no one's life keeps turning out quite the way he wants it to. Every man's life is a diary in which he plans to write one kind of story but finds himself writing some other story altogether. And we don't like that. Resentment, no matter how tightly we screw the lid on it, does pop out. The man who can't tell off his boss is liable to try to tell off his wife. She's liable to take it out on the children rather than him; they're liable to take it out on the teacher rather than her. You and I can't tell God off, can we? Instinctively we avoid that, so we keep on making certain pleasant motions toward Him and take it out on someone else, but it rankles. I've been struck by how often I've talked to people whose complaint is that their faith just doesn't mean as much to them as it used to; they just don't get much out of religion any more, and when you ask, "Well, what has happened to you lately that you're angry at God about?" at first they look outraged, but so often the question turns on some light.

Or that young salesman with his dread of coming to serious grips with God, his frank postponing of it because he knows that would be an encounter which would seriously interfere with certain ways he wants to behave—we're not all strangers to him, either, not by a long sea mile! These people who for years have been telling us that most of our faith is wishful thinking—have they really examined their doubts to see how many of them could be wishful doubting? Those who say, "Oh, religious people are fooling themselves; faith is just a form of make-believe that keeps life more endurable, more comfortable, more encouraging"—do such critics ever try the same shoe on the other foot? How often the make-believe of doubt can be comforting and encouraging! *If you are determined to live as if there were no God anywhere who cares how you live, it's very easy to find reasons why you don't believe there is one!* There is such a thing as the dread of religion, a real dread of honest-to-God religion, and our hearts know why, even if our brains don't. They know that encounter with God means no secrets left, every closet opened, every drawer ransacked, every darkness explored. All of it dragged out of storage, all we're determined to forget, the scars of our hatreds, the slow smother of our indifferences, the cheap, silly, ugly little altars we've built to our own image, our imbecile maneuverings for prestige and possession, our deliberate deceptions, our impulses to meanness. To know Someone really knows about us, and in order to help wants us to be ruthlessly honest about ourselves: it's human to dread that; even when we go through the gestures of worship we tend to hold it at arm's length. There are times when no man wants more than a nodding acquaintance with God, and there is small chance of loving Someone we think we've reason to avoid.

But it's when we speak to Bill Pierce's slim creed that we touch the core of all this. You can hope, he said, but you can't love a hope. As he looked around the universe, he could see no sure proof of a lovable God. Listen: if you could find in the sky or among the stars, on sea or land or written on the sleeve of history, any sure, undebatable proof of a lovable God, there'd have been no need for the Christian religion. There'd have been no need for One who pointed to Reality and said, "Our Father," and who, even when we killed Him, looked at us through eyes so like our own, insisting, "See Me and you've seen the Father." There are many places you can look to find traces and hints of a God you can fear, respect, wonder at, dread, but you can't find an honestly lovable God till He introduces Himself through Christ. *And even then we begin to love Him by letting Him love us.* That's how you go about it. You love God by being willing for Him to love you just as you are. Sounds easy enough, doesn't it?

Have you really tried it, you who would like to stand on your own feet and earn your own place in His eyes, a self-made soul? Have you tried, you who would like to walk up to Him with your purse in your hand, paying your share, to think of His mercy as something you've helped work out and deserve by way of a little preferential treatment? But you can't. And I can't. We'll never *earn* His favor; we're not worthy of earning it. He happens to know that you and I are rather miserable failures, but He loves us as much as if we were not failures at all. Can you understand that He feels that way about you now, that there isn't any ceremony to cleanse us, any ritual to perform, any denial with which to purify ourselves to make Him love us more than He does already? We have begun to love Him only when through mystery and through doubt, through all the questions asked since man first wondered, through all puzzling tragedy or deep sorrow, we live on the assumption that there is a God who feels that way about us now and always will.

Always will!

"There, there's a trick to tame
the gamiest soul. . . ."
—*Edna St. Vincent Millay.*

4

WHY GOD IS IN TROUBLE
WITH YOU

EDNA ST. VINCENT MILLAY died in 1950, and I confess I miss
the stiletto phrases, the sharp agnostic thrusts of that complicated little sinner as much as if they were the testimony of
a saint, because she had more respect for the religion she chose
to live in defiance of, she had more genuine admiration for
the Christ she seemed to refuse to follow, than a good many
"believers." Whenever I read the magnificent prelude music
of the creation of the world and man in Genesis, there where
the Great Baton is raised and the curtain goes up on the
Bible, I'm bound to think ever and again of the cool and
impudent wisdom of her commentary on it in one of the poems
published after her death.

When you take one of them out of its verse form, what she
says is, "I'm not overly impressed with the job God did in
creating the world. Oh, it's amazing from where I look out
at it, of course. But to turn such a trick would be routine and
simple if your power were such as God's must be. To manipulate matter, this heavy, obstinate stuff He used—it's stub-

born to be sure—but in such hands as God's it should have been easy and great fun to bend it into shape, to toss a planet here and set off a star there, and whip up a galaxy to fit them in, and even to concentrate on our little globe and decorate its crust with life! No," she argues, "if I had the wisdom and skill and strength of the Almighty I'm certain I could turn out a world at least as beautiful and brave, and as frightened and sorrowful as ours is.

"But that other trouble God got Himself into, that's what appalls me! To fashion the human heart, then set it free, turn it loose on its own and watch it go its way and turn all botched and bawdy and profligate, then try to win us back again to what He meant us for! To read our hearts as they are by now, these layers upon layers of wrong laminated in our souls like the leaves that are pressed into coal, and then try to disentangle all that without forcing us! To understand all that without hating us! To punish our wrongs without utterly destroying us! And still to keep trying to persuade our kind of wickedness to choose His kind of goodness!

"There's real trouble," she concludes. "'There's a trick to tame the gamiest soul' . . . I can't understand why He bothered in the first place, and I don't see for a moment how anything much can ever come of it. *But how I respect Him for daring to try!*"

Now, don't for a moment write that off as being too flip, too impertinent to have anything meaningful to say to us about Christian truth, for what Edna St. Vincent Millay is saying is as Biblical as the Psalms. It's far older than Moses, as up-to-the-minute as the New Testament. If we find it off-beat and shocking, it's because we're out of the habit of recognizing how shocking Christian thought really is. The Christian understanding of life has never wasted time trying to second-guess God as to why He got Himself involved in all this human experiment; neither has it ever dodged the realization that from the moment *God made man in His own image,* from that moment on God got Himself into real trouble for His pains.

Robinson Jeffers gave his sons the advice, "Be in nothing so cautious and hesitant as in your plans and hopes for mankind, for that's the trap even God caught Himself in once when He walked in a Garden, and He hasn't worked Himself out of it yet!" Of course he wrote that cynically, but there's a way in which it must be said religiously. If you see some youngster preoccupied in play on the floor, marshaling and arranging his toy soldiers in ranks for parade, ask him if he would like it if his toy soldiers should come alive. The look of excitement you'll get by way of answer may be as close as we'll ever come to sensing why God, way off in one little corner of the universe, wanted something to come alive in an odd way, alive not like the trees and the flowers with their silent and effortless obedience and praise, not like the animals that are true to the earth because they know no other home. But to come alive in at least a faint, feeble echo of the way God Himself is alive.

That's the trouble! People are not toys! They're even free to choose whether or not they shall go on being creatures of *God's* or go all out on their own. That of course will be what the boy with his toy soldiers won't realize unless he's a very unusual lad—the chance he'll be taking, the calculated risk. For what if the come-alive toys should rebel? What if they should spread their silly little legs and twist their little painted faces into an ugly snarl at him and at each other and break ranks and turn their dress parade into a dog-eat-dog affair? For that's what happened to God! That's been happening to God ever since!

Now the boy playing on the floor may think that by dint of size and strength and mind he can cuff his Lilliputians back into ranks again and keep control. But if he could do that, all it would prove is that he wants only toys. He really wants them to remain toys, just robot-brained lead soldiers that will march to his commands. That's where the whole comparison breaks down, you see. God wants a family. God wants sons and daughters who can graduate from this life to a kinship with Him that is eternal. If we have any music at all in the Christian faith, it must be some variation on that theme. If we have any story to tell, that's the main plot. God got Himself involved in all this because He wants to find in us not simply existence or obedience, *but the free, unforced recognition and response to His love.* He works for and awaits the voluntary return, fulfilled and worked out in our lives, of the will and purpose of His own heart.

Don't just blink at that! Don't pull a mental yawn at that as just so much more preacher-talk, one more load of words dumped over you, none of which seems to be quite your size, none of which seems to give pat answers to the questions you're so hungry to ask. This does get us somewhere; this gets us around at least to some hints, some thin edges of the reasons why God often deals with us the way He does.

It took a youngster a matter of seconds, this week, to send me off into a panic of unanswerables. His questions were put with that merciless directness a child uses. Why does God let Russia be what it is and do what it does? Why did God let us discover the bomb? I was so dissatisfied with my own answers all I could do for a while was to add to the list of questions. Why did God allow the agony of Hungary, that fresh, deep, nasty gash on the pulped and bleeding face of the world, right at a time when the free world was bungling so that we must stand by like some chained Samson blinded by the complexity of a day where we see the dangers but not yet the solutions? Why did God allow Little Rock? Why did

God allow that fire in that tenement, that crash on the high-way?

Suddenly in mid-flight it occurred to me that if we haven't gained on the answers, at least there has been some gain, a bare inch of progress, in the way the questions are being put. It was not so many years ago we would have been asking, from earthquake to pestilence to war to personal disaster, why did God do this? Why did God Himself do this? It's a gain on wisdom to be asking instead, "Why does God *allow* this?" For that makes some room for faith's realization that *earth's or our own unhappiness comes not by God's intention, but with God's reluctant permission.*

And there's even a chink to be found, a peephole peering into the reasons for that reluctant permission, whenever we remind ourselves that the world is made up of people very much, oh, very much, like you and me. Some of them are much better. Some of them are much worse, but they're all enough like you and me that *the trouble God has with them is recognizably the same trouble God is in with us.*

You probably read in the newspaper of an incident which puts it as neatly and succinctly as anything I've ever heard. A waitress was taking orders from a couple at the table and their young son; she was one of the class of veteran waitresses who never show outright disrespect to their customers, but who frequently make it quietly evident by their unhurried pace and their level stare that they fear no mortal, not even parents. She jotted on her order pad deliberately and silently as the father and mother gave their luncheon selection and gratuitous instructions as to what was to be substituted for what, and which dressing changed to what sauce. When she finally turned to the boy, he began his order with a kind of fearful desperation. "I want a hot dog—" he started. And both parents barked at once, "No hot dog!" The mother went on,

"Bring him the lyonnaise potatoes and the beef, both vegetables and a hard roll and—" The waitress wasn't even listening. She said evenly to the youngster, "What do you want on your hot dog?" He flashed an amazed smile, "Ketchup, lots of ketchup, and—and bring a glass of milk." "Coming up," she said as she turned from the table, leaving behind her the stunned silence of utter parental dismay. The boy watched her go before he turned to his father and mother with astonished elation to say, *"You know what? She thinks I'm real!"* She thinks I'm real.

I'm not certain exactly where that belongs in the disciplines of a human family. Perhaps we discover exactly where only with our grandchildren! I'm not wise enough to know where it does and does not apply in education, for there it so often seems to have become a sentimentality rather than a wisdom. But there isn't any doubt where it belongs in religion—dead center! Right at the heart! *For that's the trouble God's in with you. He thinks you're real!* He has placed you in a life where you can order hot dogs whether they're good for you or not. Yes, and get them! He pays you that almost intolerable compliment: He thinks you're real, that you're a person. That's why He'll do everything He possibly can to win you for the kind of person He knows you can become, everything except violate your right to choose and seek and decide.

Oh, He'll bless us in a thousand ways we don't deserve and may not even notice. He'll plead with us and warn us in a thousand others. He'll call to us by "Prophet, Book and Martyr." He'll even step down into Galilee and in the inside story of Christmas, the real story of what began at Christmas, He'll show us things and tell us things in this Christ that no one has ever been able to look at or listen to since without at least wishing that it were true. He'll even show you a cross where He looked at us through His pain and died for us! Here's a

God who'll do even that for us. But He will not dissolve the grit in our souls by forcing on us a way of life we really don't want to believe or live, by forcing on us a destiny we're really not seeking.

Edna Millay was right about it. *"There's a trick to tame the gamiest soul."* To win us by treating us not like puppets but sons: that's why, time and time again, He must just keep hands off, just stand there and watch and wait. Paul Scherer reminds us how often we've seen a human father do it—leave some angry child to itself before he can win the child back again. As he waits, the father remembers the early years when his hands dared to guide the child's first uncertain steps, and he longs for the day when this sulking disobedience will have spent itself, and he denies every deep impulse to sweep the child fiercely back into his arms now. But for the moment he waits.

Love with its eyes wide open, forcing itself to keep quiet, to stay out of this for the moment. Letting us fail if we're determined to—that's our privilege!—but caring, desperately caring, wanting so to help! Respecting us too much to interfere, until we really decide we want things to go His way, until we really, honestly want His help, until He's really asked!

. . . Of Jacob and Jacob's ladder: "You can dish up that sort of dream any time from the right ingredients of loneliness, indigestion and conscience. . . ."

—*Uncle Walter*

5

LOUNGING ON THE ALTAR

I HAD AN UNCLE who could explain anything, at least to his own complete satisfaction. He was my talking uncle, a distinction that had to be fought for again and again in our family circle. He was the first vividly to illustrate to my childhood the rigors of the truth that there are two kinds of guests, those who bring happiness wherever they go, and those who bring happiness whenever they go! This uncle was pre-eminent at family reunions, often challenged but never outdone, our own Ancient Mariner who, with glittering eye as signal and index finger flourished like a baton, held forth explaining everything.

Of course he was at his best explaining away the Bible. Our anxious mother usually shooed our innocent ears out of range when he began his Bible discourses. It was a strangely coveted badge of maturity when at last you were allowed to remain and hear the tragicomedy of this typical American phenomenon, the cracker-barrel Clarence Darrow, who because he had sinned a sin or two and had seemed to get by with it, and because he had read a book or two and had never recovered

43

from it, and because he was cursed with what is poisonously termed "the gift of gab," was forever ready by day and by night to give the waiting universe his explanations of everything.

And of course he made short work of Jacob's ladder. Since this famed Bible scene is a universal children's favorite, we were all aghast at Uncle Walter's brief dismissal of it: "Just a dream," he would say. "Just a lad's dream, saved from being a nightmare by wishful thinking. After all," he would go on, "Jacob was the Old Testament's Tom Sawyer, an attractive rascal who lived by his wits, tricking and sponging off of everyone in sight. Here he was running for his life to get away from the brother he had fleeced, and he spends the night in this wild, strange wood, stones for a pillow and a very raw young conscience for a bed. Of course, he dreamed he saw angel traffic on a golden stair. Of course he dreamed he heard God speaking fulsome comforts and promises. You can dish up the same sort of dream any time from the right ingredients of loneliness, indigestion, and conscience. That's all it was. They shouldn't bother mature people with it." Such was the gospel according to Uncle Walter.

I bother you with him only because he was and is such a stock type. It is astonishing that after so many years of such disdain from these terrible belittlers, that *these ancient scenes continue to speak a message to mature people that can be heard from no other source.* Every alert mind has the task somehow of going beyond the world's Uncle Walters, to find new levels of the Bible's message. This story of Jacob, for example, can charm a child *as a story,* but adult eyes must look beyond the charm and through the story for a truth that is far from childish.

That truth will always be inescapably personal. That's the true key to the Scriptures—the realization that these are not just stories told concerning other people long ago, but are dramas in which you and I are cast. The Bible is written about you and me. Every scene is a pointed finger. It isn't just a lad named Jacob who cheats his brother and runs away. We do that in a thousand ways, and so much of our life is a flight. And yet, for us too, if we're ever alerted to it, above our uneasy beds there always opens the ladder, that mysterious channel of give and take between us and a watching God.

Or, believe it, there will be no headline tomorrow morning that will have as much to do with you and me as this Jacob said when he awakened from his dream in fear. He knew enough to find more than mere comfort in his dream. He knew that in his runaway camping expedition, he had blundered into the Presence of God. There he had slouched himself down, thinking it an ordinary place, when all the while there was something terribly sacred about it; it was one of those ordinary places where God breaks into life! *"Surely the Lord is in this place and I knew it not!"* he said. For he had been slouching in a chancel, if you please, sprawling in a shrine somehow, *lounging on an altar*. And it's a great day for you and me when we awaken with the same alarm, when we come to see that all through life our gravest danger is that we lounge on the altars. When we're aware of that, then our great tomorrows are born.

You'll hear it said that one of the things basically wrong with us today is that the idea of the Holy has dropped through some crack in the bottom of our thinking and has quite disappeared, that no longer for most Americans are there holy places and sacred names and awe-inspiring customs which we seriously revere. If that's true, it is a terrifying truth. For the man who has nothing before which he is eager to bow will some day be flattened by the sheer weight of himself.

Dr. W. E. Sangster tells of being present at an anniversary

celebration in Gloucester which gathered many dignitaries. One clergyman on the rostrum was most impressive not only because of the portliness of his figure and the red and black velvet on his robe, but also for a striking gold cross he wore suspended from a heavy watch chain. Sangster mentions his horror on noticing all through the principal speaker's address that the portly clergyman, obviously bored by anyone's efforts but his own, had taken the golden cross from his chain and was cleaning his fingernails with a corner of it! We've all been in danger of that unconcern in the Christian Church of the latter days, laymen and cleric alike—with our loose thinking and our trifling with so much that the centuries have known was serious, with Sunday so obviously just another day, and the church just another competing organization, with worship become mostly sermon-tasting, with our amazing flabbiness in the disciplines of prayer and usefulness that alone can make God real to men! We've been sending faith on pretty errands trying to harness its eternal claims to cure our headache or give us more poise, stripping the gospel down to a mere Biblical barbiturate, a two-for-a-nickel sedative packaged for peace of mind! In all this we present inheritors of the Christian tradition stand perilously close to just that brand of irreverence —cleaning our fingernails with the cross.

And yet, for all that, and the danger of all that, it is not our gravest danger. We all should now and then back off and stare at this a moment. Jesus of Nazareth lived among people who had a magnificent notion of the Holy with their Sabbath observances, their disciplines of prayer and sacrifice, their dead earnestness about every needle and pin of worship! Surely, among the Jews Christ knew, we find reverence made a high art. Surely, they were the supreme churchmen of history. Yet it was at these people Christ aimed the cutting edges of His crusade. It was these high churchmen who killed Him, who couldn't endure Him, who had to have Him out of the way. For here was Christ's simple, basic, revolutionary insistence about what is sacred in life, something that a child could see but enough to terrify a saint. In Elton Trueblood's paraphrase, *Faith lives or dies not by what goes on in churches, but by what, as a result of churches, goes on outside of them.* Don't, says Christ (whether to the Pharisee or to us), don't see religion as primarily what goes on in some peculiar building with pointed arches and stained-glass windows. That building is the necessary schoolhouse, the pulsing heart, the arsenal, the moment's retreat, the place of prayer, the house of spoken praise, the assembly hall for the town meeting of some family of God. But religion is the manner in which all the ordinary enterprises of daily living are conducted. Because God is involved in all of it, He is met and dealt with in the way we work, the way we entertain, the way we make love, the way we think, the way we laugh, the way we complain, the way we dream and the way we die! God is in all that. He is praised and served or mocked and opposed in how we handle all that. We are God's only when we try to find His hidden glory somewhere in everything we do.

Have you ever taken this Christian religion up in both hands to stare at it that way? To realize that's what Christ is talking about? Well, that isn't couched in King James' phrases, but believe it, for that's part of what they killed Him for, for saying, "You priests, you people, as you stroll from your very temple, this is your tragedy. *All life is a church. And you've been sprawling in its chancel, you've been lounging on its altars.* All life is a church and you keep blundering into God's presence without even knowing He's there."

You, Dives, didn't you hear that sharp intake of breath as of Someone watching in horror, didn't you catch that faint rustle like the quick retreat of angel wings when you kicked the beggar Lazarus outside your door this morning? Church was going on out there at the curb, man, and you knew it not.

You good people of the town who dragged through the dust that adulteress yesterday ready to stone her, your faces blotched with self-righteous anger, your eyes a bewildering study in primitive delight in another mortal's shame! What a chance was yours for sympathy and help! But no! Didn't you hear the organ play, as she huddled there on the ground before you? A sacrament was being offered you, and you knew it not.

You elder brother of the prodigal, when you came in from work the other night and found the lad had come home, a scared, hurt, burned shell of a boy who had learned the hard way that the flesh cannot live for the flesh! When your father asked you too to come and throw your arms around him, and you spat on that moment—didn't you feel the shock of something, hear the ripping of some golden fabric, as if a priest had called you to prayer and you had mouthed a curse instead? Why, that was a moment of pure worship, man, and you knew it not.

Or you Levite, you temple official, rushed as you were on the road last week when you saw that man hurt and needing help. Of course he was on the other side of the road from you, but you were near enough to see his wounds, near enough to see his face. As you passed by and turned your head away, knowing someone else would stop, didn't the sky darken a little? Didn't there come some hint of harshness in the breeze? Wasn't there some lackluster to the day as if something which could have been fine now couldn't be? You see, in that hurt stranger life was taking up the offering, and you knew it not.

That's what He still says. He hasn't changed one syllable of it. All life is a church. Quit profaning its altars! And it's a question whether He'll bother to go on saying that too much longer to a people that stays as careless about it all as we do.

And Jacob awaked out of his sleep. There was fear in his eyes but also the lingering touch of a dream upon his heart. Perhaps the fear is the price of the dream, as long as men are like Jacob. And we are like Jacob. And what is there to it all unless we awaken and bet our lives that Christ is right? Otherwise it's all an unasked-for jumble of men and tasks and dirt and cold steel and clay, and short pleasures and long pains, and a little love and much sorrow, and a few friends and a long loneliness. Or it's a venture for brave and simple men, an enterprise that is God-filled, with a living God to be met or evaded, acknowledged or resisted at every turn of the road.

The choice is not ours as to whether we'll do business with Him, any more than we can choose whether to breathe or not, since wherever you turn, *there's an altar. In God's name, how could we be casual about any of it ever again, once Christ has opened our eyes to that!*

"... Who was He? *Who was He?* Or won't we ever know? Is that the judgment of Nazareth, that we will never know?"

—*The Shopkeeper*

6

WHAT THE SHOPKEEPER TOLD
THE STRANGERS

THE STRANGERS COULD not have been certain Benjamin had noticed them standing there outside the freshly whitewashed shop, eyeing with more of a stranger's surprise than customer's interest the variety and profusion of the wares displayed in the colorful clutter of this wayside bazaar. You did not expect to find at the side of any road, here in backwoods Galilee, quite so ambitious a market-place, and it was evident that the nearby village of itself could not have supported or justified it. For here and there, in the expected display of native necessities, half an eye could catch the gleam of luxury goods. Those baskets looked Egyptian in design, and those cheeses were unmistakably Bithynian, those sandals suggested the leatherwork of Laodicea, those veils would be from Arabia and those shirts perhaps Cilicia. While under the adjoining tent where the girl was tending the small food mart, those fish she was weighing would of course be salted and brought over from the lake, and the honey-cured figs hanging on the posts were surely brought up from the south.

51

The strangers could not have been certain Benjamin had
noticed them standing out there, *but that was only because
they did not know Benjamin the Samaritan.* They could not
know that with his gift for multiple awareness, which he
claimed only a misplaced Samaritan could develop, Benjamin
was somehow able to watch how carefully his daughter was
weighing and marketing the salted fish, at the same time that
he inventoried his supplies to check whether those light-
fingered camel traders had stolen more than they purchased
last night, at the same time that he was considering whether
to re-order so soon the jugs and basins from Sidon that were
going unexpectedly well, at the same time that he watched the
road through a slit of a window and had spotted the strangers
all the way down the path from the hillside village of Nazareth. From back in the shop, as he seemed still to rummage,
he was looking them over now. Yes, they were the same, no
mistaking the pair who had stopped here three days ago asking where they might find rooms and food in Nazareth town.
They were an odd pair to visit Nazareth. The young Greek,
the dark one, dressed as he was in walking sandals and a
rough tunic practical for travel, had something about his ease
and assurance of manner that didn't agree with the small white
scar on his ear which his finger tips stroked occasionally, the
scar which told the world he had sometime been branded and
sold as a slave. He acted quite the equal of the other, the
Roman, who was somewhat older, though it was hard to judge
the age of these Romans, with their close-cropped hair and
clean-shaved jaw, walking as they all did straight as cedars,
heads back as befitted these conquerors of the world. Yet this
one looked without arrogance; he even seemed to see what he
looked at, and his dress puzzled Benjamin. Those linens he
wore were fine-spun, richly textured, the best—but no jeweled
cuffs, no embroidered hem to his coat, no silver inlay on the

broad leather belt at his waist. What would so unlikely a pair be doing up here in the mountains of Nazareth? Benjamin allowed himself the early morning luxury of a quick smile of vast amusement at himself. The inventory and the order to Sidon must wait. Business was business, and he'd wager a drachma he wouldn't sell these Gentiles so much as one honey-puffed fig. *But curiosity was also curiosity.*

He walked out to greet them with none of the antic and overdone welcome of some bowing and scraping rug merchant, but with just a nod and a quizzical smile while the eyes beneath his craggy brows were not lowered, even with the nod. He had looked too many men in the face here at the crossroads to bow too low to anyone before he had to. Even then, you couldn't be certain Benjamin's bow would be very low!

"Welcome back to the wayside peddlar's diggings, my distinguished strangers! My only surprise is that you've stayed away so long. If you've need of anything of quality, of taste, it is not to be found in Nazareth, in that rabbit-warren of shops and marts around the village well. My competitors there are so busy shoving each other for standing room and haggling over breathing space that they've overlooked the little matter of having something to sell. Yes, Nazareth is picturesque enough as you see it from here, like a toy town against the hillside. Look at it up there in the morning sun and you'd swear the synagogue is new and that the houses are gleaming as if just scrubbed, framed in that luxury of cypress groves and the silver and gold excitement of the olive trees and vineyards. It's only when you're nearer that the magic vanishes and you see it for what it is, just another ingrown Galilean townlet, a fit nest for boors and bumpkins who'll be content as their fathers were with dried clay huts and roofs of wattled palm leaves. They've made a proverb of it in the cities, you know—

'Can any good come out of—?' But here I stand, rattling away the morning, when I know it was some errand brought you back to Benjamin's. Some recognizable foodstuffs, say, to take back to the Inn so that you'll know what you're eating? Or a vintage wine? I've some from Cyprus, to replace that local swill they've served you. Or that sour red from Sharon which I swear they press from wilted roses? No? A gift, then; would that be it? Some souvenir of this trek of yours—by the prophets, I've a piece of work from a goldsmith in Antioch, bought it off a trader's caravan last week; haven't shown it to a customer yet, and it's as choice a—No? How can I help you then?

"What? You're after *information?* Gentlemen, forgive my amusement, but you are rather obviously citizens of the world. There could be slim doubt that you've discovered long since that there is no commodity come by so cheaply as Galilean gossip, that half a shaved shekel will loose the tongue of the nearest flea-bitten camel driver to tell all he knows and even more that he doesn't. What could we of backwoods Nazareth know that would bring such as you to ferret it out? Who? Say it again. But of course! Of course! No, they wouldn't talk to you up in the village about Him, would they now? Why my wits are as slow as an Idumean ox! Come on in back, through the storeroom if you would. No, on through the open door. Forgive me if I close it behind us. You'd honor me by being seated. Oh, take your choice, I'll stand, if I may; peddlars think clearer on their feet, you know. Of course they'd clam up, in the village. They took you for spies, and not even the clink of your coins would help. But you're not from the temple crowd in Jerusalem; they'd hire no Gentiles. I've a hunch that you're not spying for Herod or the Roman police. The way you said His name!

"Yes, I knew Jesus of Nazareth. How long? That's hard to

say. I was older than He of course, but that's an odd one.
You never thought of Him as being one age or another. Can't
remember when I first became aware of Him. He was just
always around, another Nazarene, part of the local scenery. I
suppose it was when we first began to handle the wooden
plows and rakes and spades He made, when He took over
Joseph's trade. We were more of an outlet to the farmers
through the valley than He could be at the shop in town. He
was head of the family by then, and hard as He worked it
was touch and go those years, for He was a craftsman; He
turned out finished work, none of this shoddy stuff that warps
in the first dew or splits at the first strain. He knew wood—
He had a feel for the curve of the grain; the joints He made
held! I remember when He'd fashion yoke for oxen, He had to
know the size of the brutes that would wear it, a tailor-made
yoke if you please, because He insisted that when a yoke fits,
then it seems easy, and the burden light!

"Yes, He was odd; no, that word won't do. 'Different' is
the word, but different in a different way. He was one of us
but something more that you could never name nor point to.
People wondered how He could work so hard and yet have so
much time for the children who flocked to His shop to listen
to His stories as He worked. I knew why. Everything He
told you He made you not just hear but see. Not that He'd
talk much to the rest of us, except man to man. That's what
surprised us so, later. He did His work and went His way,
and you could see He was watching and listening—and waiting, I always thought, waiting for something.

"Oh, I talked to Him. We were lonely, our family. Pros-
perous and lonely. To a Jew you know, we are not Jews, we
Samaritans. We're worse than you are; we're Gentiles pretending to be Jews. Of half-caste, heathen ancestry, they say; it
makes no difference if we can quote Moses by the scroll, obey

the Torah to the letter. God just hasn't any time for us, only
for them. Well, from the looks of them they could do with a
little less of the full divine attention! We were never accepted,
only tolerated, for we were their peddlars, their only contact
with the world of trade up here. But this Jesus—you know I
told Him once of a trip I had made down the Jericho road to
check the date crops. I found a man on the road, badly hurt,
been there some time, and that's a busy highway; people just
wouldn't bother to stop and help. I told Him about it and I
never saw Him so excited. I can still feel the iron grip of His
hand on my arm, as He looked at me and said, 'The priests
passed him by and the levites passed him, but you, the Good
Samaritan. . . !' No one had ever called me that! No one
ever made me feel like that.

"I didn't know how fond I was of Him, how much I'd miss
Him, till He was gone. Who was it who said that someone
can mean so much to us but we never give a thought to how
much until they aren't around any more. It's in the years since
that I've realized He proved to me you can combine strength
and tenderness. They don't mix, you know; but He *joined*
them. I've seen Him drive a spike down to the head in some
tough joist with one rippling-armed hammer blow, just as He
could drive some truth through your heart with one word.
But He faced men with tenderness, as if He saw beneath all
our ugliness the sick child in everyman's heart which He
wanted to take in His arms and comfort back to health. I've
realized since He's the only man I ever knew who could talk
of God without posing, without making some kind of face.
You know what I mean; the Pharisee looks strained and holy,
most of us look embarrassed and awkward, or the blasphemer
looks like a pouting child who has just told off his parents,
when the name of God is mentioned.

"But not Jesus. Do you know, I thought for so long He was

talking about Joseph, when He'd mention His Father so
naturally. But He wasn't talking about Joseph. Oh, there was
quite a stir when He left, without a word to anyone. I kept
thinking, 'Well, whatever He was waiting for, it came.' Then
we began to hear those rumors.

"Fantastic incredible stories of what He was saying and
doing over by the lake and in the villages. Teaching huge
crowds of people—that wasn't His style, and yet, the way those
children used to flock to His shop. Healing people, it couldn't
be! And yet—the way He saw the sick child in all our hearts!
He came back once. Only once. Have you heard of that visit?
What? Yes, the day He showed up in the little synagogue. I
wasn't there of course; they wouldn't have let me in. But I
guess it was quite a moment. He just sat there in the synagogue
(full that morning, believe me), as if He had nothing to say;
so the old Rabbi asked Him to read the lesson of the morning.
He took the scroll and read from Isaiah, 'The Spirit of the
Lord is upon me, because he hath anointed me to preach the
gospel to the poor; he hath sent me to heal the brokenhearted,
to preach deliverance to the captives, and recovering of sight
to the blind, to set at liberty them that are bruised, To preach
the acceptable year of the Lord.' Then He put down the
scroll and faced them and said quietly, 'This day is this
Scripture fulfilled in your ears.' They were beside themselves,
of course; the place broke into an uproar. 'You!' they hooted.
'You, the carpenter, Mary's son? It was of you Isaiah spoke?
You will make the blind see?' And He said, 'Not in Nazareth.'
He walked down this very road later, when He left for good.
I saw Him. I wanted to rush out to Him and tell Him there
was one who'd miss Him. But there was something about Him
held me back, as if He no longer belonged to us. Near my
tent there He turned and looked back up the hill at Nazareth,
the little synagogue, the houses, where those bumpkins lived

who were too small to see anyone bigger than they were.
Wouldn't you think there'd have been hurt pride and resentment and bitterness on His face and in His eyes? Well, there
was not a trace. He stood there looking and I stood watching,
and there was nothing in His eyes and on His face as He
looked back at Nazareth but understanding and love. Then
He walked down the road to the lake, and the shadow He
cast seemed to grow as He walked.

"You wanted information. How absurd! Why don't you tell
me? Who was He? *Who was He?* Or won't we ever know?
Is that the judgment of Nazareth, that we will never know?"

". . . I could have emptied every slum and farmyard from Hebron to Kadesh in thirty days for His army; there's not a true son of Israel from Beer-sheba to Zebulun would not have sold his last tattered cloak to help. But no. He'd have none of it. . . ."

—*Judas Iscariot*

7

REQUIEM FOR A TREASURER

THE MAN MUST have slipped into the room while Ben-hanan
was at the window. Perhaps he had been there at the window
longer than he realized, pulling aside the stiff gold-brocaded
drapes, and peering into the north to see if this merciless
crashing of the thunder, this continuous rip of the lightning,
meant anything. How could you tell? Was the storm abating
or was it still gathering force? Ben-hanan swore a precise and
scholarly, priestly oath in just the proper liturgical phrases as
he stood there. He couldn't remember such a storm as this in
the middle of the day, in Jerusalem. It was so black out there
that except for the blazing crooked javelins of lightning, he
couldn't even see the tower of the Roman garrison which
stood not a hundred yards away. How was he to get to work
in all this? He'd never be ready in time for his full report to
the Treasurer's Council. If he kept the drapes pulled against
the rain the room was a gasping steam bath. Yet, pull them
apart and ignore the rain and that wind would slap out every
lamp he had lighted. And what was there about this storm
that kept luring him to leave the neat rows of figures on his

61

desk to stare out there *where you'd think the very God of Sinai were dying of heartbreak,* out there where His sacred city seemed to be the target for nature's own frenzy of mourning—those boiling clouds a monstrous funeral dance, and that howling wind a wild and savage dirge shrieked to the drum roll of the thunder till your hackles stood at the sound of it.

But what foolishness was this, for the high priest's own brother to be brooding at a window like some Samaritan witch? Weariness did this to the brain, weariness from too much excitement and loss of sleep. He had been hauled from bed last night by the excitement over that stubborn Nazarene. His whole morning had been wasted at Pilate's palace. What a Passover this had been! How glad he'd be to see it over.

But at least it had not disrupted the flow of temple revenues. Thanks to the God of Jacob, there was one thing left in the world you could depend on. Feast days meant pilgrims by the thousands, and pilgrims by the thousands meant offerings by the barrel, and offerings meant a good report for the Treasurer's Council. That was the comforting thing about money. Men might go mad and dream they were Messiahs. The world might go mad and blot out the sun with a noonday storm. But money neither dreamed nor stormed. So long as you could count it, you knew you could count on it. And smiling Ben-hanan turned from the window, then froze there. How could this man have slipped into the room? How could he get past the guards downstairs—but of course, this storm! And wasn't he—yes, he was that spy named Judas, the informer from the town Kerioth. But why should he be sitting motionless on the scribe's bench there at the deskside? A flash outside flared on his face and hands—what was that in his hands? Judas let a full moment drag by before he spoke, in a low key, but with such intensity that it carried above the thunder.

"The storm has flushed all the rats from the gutters, my noble Ben-hanan. They creep even into the temple. Or did you notice it was storming? Did you wonder, when you saw how drenched I am, why? Did you think, *'What a pity; the priest's friend, Israel's brave benefactor, has been out in the rain'?* How do you know this is rain, Ben-hanan? Isn't there something thicker than water that can drench a man's cloak? Don't raise your voice for a guard, now. You could shriek your sacred, dedicated lungs out to no purpose in this bedlam. And there's no guard at your door. They've gone, deserted! You know, I'm somewhat of an authority on desertion. And don't even cut your eyes toward that other door. Haven't you ever heard of the speed of the desperate and the strength of the damned? We move like cats, you know, like cornered cats; we can see in the dark because we're afraid of the light.

"It's very wise of you to look frightened, Ben-hanan. Never be afraid of the man who has something to lose. Save your fears for those of us who have nothing to win, here or ever. No, come on to your desk. You've my word, and you know how good that is, that I'll not harm you so long as you remain so gracious and accommodating a host. After all, I've taken no small risk and gone quite out of my way to pay you a professional visit. We two treasurers, you know, should have much in common. This money pouch I'm carrying is the bond that makes us, dare I say, blood brothers? Why do you stare at it? It's no more tainted than the shekels you've shoveled into your bins all week—oh! It wasn't the money bag you shrank from? It was *this?* Why, this is a whip, gentle priest, a whip or a rope, whichever you need at a given moment, and there are so many uses for both! Look how well it's made;

it's braided of rawhide thongs. A clever craftsman made it, with strong, quick, able hands, hands that by now are— Ben-hanan, look out of your window. It faces north, doesn't it? How far can you see? Yes, with the lightning, can—can you see outside the city walls? Can you see as far as the—execution grounds? Are there any signs of the crowd returning?

"No! Sit down, I don't need to look. I can see it plainer than anyone who was there. Listen to that thunder! It is thunder isn't it? It can't last much longer; there isn't much time. I must make up my mind what I'm going to say if I get there before He does, if I get to tell my story first. But isn't that singular? That's why I'm here, and only now do I realize it. I tried to break into Caiaphas' house to return this money. I thought I came here on the same final errand, but I see I really came to tell someone why. To tell someone of your family, your dynasty of priests, whom Israel calls so well the hissing adders, that I joined forces with you. Not because I'm one of you. I'm not your stripe of snake, Ben-hanan. That's the only epitaph I want. But isn't it amazing? You take an evil heart and peel off its blackness layer by layer like some monstrous onion and when you reach the core of the thing and there should be nothing left, there is something left. There is one scrap of pride, one voice that keeps whimpering that I was justified in what I did. And that voice must rehearse its story to some human ear to see if even I can believe it, before I try to beat Him Beyond, to tell my story first, to argue with those thunders.

"But how will you understand, you who wear that priestly purple because you do business with Rome? How could I make you feel what it's like so to love Israel and so to hate Rome that the love and the hatred are twin flames of the same fire? You were never as a child snatched just in time from before the Roman chariot wheels as you played in your village streets. Your first hot, searing memory wouldn't be mine—that look on arrogant Roman faces as they glanced back at your screams and laughed. Were your only boyhood fantasies the silly daydreams of what Samson would do, what Gideon would do, what David would do if he were here today? Did you come into manhood with but one thirst, one quest?

"How long—how long will the God of Abraham forget His people? First the perfumed Syrian, then the precious delicate Greeks, now these Roman pigs, all with their feet on Israel's neck. My hatred of them cost me Miriam, the only beauty, the only gentleness that finally would look my way. But she was a fool as the gentle are all fools! She said that terrible thing to me that day I left her, 'You do not love Israel, Judas, just as you do not love me. Love to you is but a mirror in which you try to see your own reflection, your own hard triumphant face.' Why would she have said that? But the gentle always talk in riddles. He—He talked in riddles too. But when I first saw Him—you saw Him this morning, at the trial. Ever see Him before? No? Ever hear Him speak? I've watched Him hold five thousand motionless, as if by some magic He had drawn their breath. I've watched Him walk into a village and take over that village without so much as a gesture. I've seen Him stand on a wind-blown hill in Galilee, and that hill became a throne, and the sunlight on His hair a crown, and every peasant in the crowd a legionnaire. And I knew He was what I had waited for, that this power must not be wasted. Oh, it was a struggle not to fall under His spell myself. He was a wizard, when you looked Him in the eyes! I never knew quite what color to call His eyes.

"No, it was when I was alone I'd break His spell each night. I would unlearn what He had taught me. I would confess my creed: 'Blessed are the crafty for they shall inherit the earth. Blessed are the ruthless for they can enforce the right. Blessed

are they that cherish their resentments, they shall wield the
whip in the day of retribution. If there's to be power there
cannot be love. If there's to be wisdom there cannot be love.
Where there is sorrow, that debt can't be cleared with love.
Blessed is Judas who will make the Messiah in his own
image.' For three years I wove my own spell to keep myself
safe inside from His spell—for three years, with those fishermen of His, as stupid as their own carp, that clod Simon, that
poet-dreamer John, that lippy Thomas. I took it because I had
plans—for Jesus. I had my own plans, too, great plans. Don't
you see it Ben-hanan? I didn't betray Him. *He betrayed me!*
He betrayed me! Didn't He? He wouldn't organize. Time and
again one slight word from Him and the crowds would have
proclaimed Him King! I could have emptied every slum and
farmyard from Hebron to Kadesh in thirty days for His army;
there's not a true son of Israel from Beer-sheba to Zebulun
would not have sold his last tattered cloak to help. But no.
He'd have none of it. Riddles and evasions. He even grew
unwilling to be seen so much in public. His crowds began to
fall away from Him.

"I knew this Passover at Jerusalem was our last chance.
When would there be another? Rome is busy across the world,
fighting the Gauls. We know that Pilate is short of men in
Judea. If the thousands of us who thronged Jerusalem this
week had raised the banner of revolt, Israel could have been
free before the news reached Rome. Oh, twice I thought I had
won. Once, on the Sabbath when the pilgrims along the road
caught up a marching song and swept Him through the city
gates in triumph. And then in the very temple here, when He
took this rope, this very rawhide whip, and led that mob scene
in your courtyard, smashing the cages of the sacrificial doves,
scattering the neatly stacked coins of your short-change artists
at their booths, with fire in His eyes and that slogan on His

lips which the crowd caught up as they joined Him, 'Den of Thieves, Den of Thieves, My Father's House a Den of Thieves.' And you priests trembled, and even the Roman guards at the gates stood paralyzed at the fury of it. I saw it then, Ben-hanan, what I had lived to see, *fear in the eyes of Romans!* But then He withdrew. Right at the moment when it all could have roared into revolt, He simply walked away from a throne!

"It was then I knew I had to force His hand. The timing was perfect; it was God-given. It couldn't fail. To turn Him over to you. To trick you into arresting Him in the dead of night, then spread the word that Caiaphas and Pilate had seized their prophet. That would do it. They'd never stand for that. Barabbas still has a thousand armed guerillas hiding in these hills. Others would swarm with the very wind. But the mob could carry the first charge alone. They'd never let Rome crucify their. . . .

"What went wrong, Ben-hanan? You from your side, tell me! Was this His final treachery to me, that my big plan simply fitted one little corner of His plans? Did—did you get the same notion at the trial this morning that I got over across the brook last night? That this somehow is His triumph, that He's somehow in charge, that He had maneuvered all of us, that He willed to be hanging out there now as surely as if He Himself had driven the nails through His own. . . .

"But you can see why I'm returning this money, can't you? Can't you? It's no affair of mine really, this bribe business. You won't take it? Then there it is by the handful on your holy floor, silver seed for a bloody harvest, treasurer! This wasn't my doing; why, it's as if I'd made great plans for a friend and discovered I'd been toying with God Himself. Oh, I didn't mean to say that. That's something the demons have whispered to me since dawn. But that would be an unthinkable

horror. To have talked and walked and lived with and have
given the kiss of death to. . . .

"Listen—where's the thunder? Is the storm—no, I'll look.
Oh, God of Jacob, it's nearly over, He'll get there first. He'll
get to tell His story first. This is a good whip, Ben-hanan,
good as a whip or good as a rope, and those who live by the
whip might as well—Oh, but wouldn't that be terrible! I
never knew what color to call His eyes. What if, when I get
there, I'd find myself telling my story not to the thunders or
the lightnings, but to those gentle, terrible, wide-open eyes?
But I've got to know. I've got to know now! Keep the money,
Ben-hanan. As one treasurer to another, I think you'll need
it, lots of it. I—I won't."

". . . only then did I get this feeling I haven't been able to shake, that this was not my execution squadron and not yours, that Someone else was in command, that we weren't dragging Him up that hill, that staggering and stumbling as He did, He was leading us. . . ."

—*The Centurion*

8

ONE SOLDIER'S PRAYER ONE
FRIDAY NIGHT

THE YOUNGER SOLDIER stood at the one large window of the room, bathing. He sponged off his body with the fresh water from the copper basin the slave had brought, and deliberately let its coolness pour down over his thirsty skin, turning now and then to stand erect in the window while the unseasonable breeze that had followed the thunderstorm played over his body. Every tired, cramped muscle seemed to demand that he miss no moment of that fresh, cool air, but stand there fairly chilling in the luxury of it.

Here from the second floor of the Roman garrison you could tell the storm was passing, even though the rain still pelted down, for the gloom was thinning overhead, and the sunset sky showed an apricot hue patchworked by refugee shreds of cloud running before the wind that soon would sweep it clean. He hoped this didn't mean a return of the heat tomorrow.

Why, Varro thought, he would rather face the howling barbarians in pitched battle on any frontier of the empire any day than take on another crucifixion detail, such as today's.

And the veterans in the barracks here had told him it would be mere routine!

He glanced along the cleanly whitewashed wall of the room to the far corner where he had so wearily dumped his gear when he undressed. It was hard to believe that sweat-grimed crumpled rag had been a clean red dress-parade tunic this morning, or that his shoulder plates had gleamed as armour should. Even the reddish tuft of horsehair on his helmet, which proudly proclaimed him a centurion, was dust-caked and bedraggled.

What a morning and what an afternoon! Varro rubbed his shoulder muscles ruefully, and wondered half aloud if it were possible for a man to roast alive, really to bake in his own armour under such a sun as had blazed for hours out on that ugly little hill.

He'd better get the orderly to work shining that armour at once. Tomorrow he'd be back on patrol duty, rattling Rome's weapons in the face of these strange Jews. "Full combat attire" had been posted as the order for the week, so long as such a mob was in Jerusalem and the temper of the people so ugly.

He had just stepped from the basin to gather up his clothes when the other soldier, an older man who had been lying on one bunk, his hands behind his head and his eyes closed, sat up, swinging his feet with the same motion in a heavy weariness to the floor, and spoke testily. "Well, have you finished your marathon bath, Commander Varro? From the splashing and the sighing I thought perhaps you fancied yourself a Greek. Or were you waiting for the daughters of Jerusalem to come back into the streets that you might flex your biceps at them like some brawn-brained gladiator? Dress, man, dress! I've seen enough of flesh today!"

Varro started back more in surprise than annoyance, and more at the tone than the words, for the banter was barracks

routine. But in the five weeks they had been quartered together here, this was the first time Centurion Longinus had
turned on him the bite of a tongue of which all the garrison
was wary. Longinus stood from the bunk now, stretched not
so much in leisure as in obvious impatience, then walked
to the window, kicked the basin clanging aside with careful
aim from his loosely sandaled foot, and stared out the window
before he glanced back.

"I'm sorry, Varro. You're hardly the one to take it out on, if
I'm as surly tonight as some old Scythian bear. Why is it that
at your age temper shows spirit, but at my age all it shows
is that you're older than you care to feel? There, that's better,
that grin fits the shape of your face far better than a battle
glare.

"What are you hunting? Why, that's a fresh towel there at
my bunk. No, No. Go ahead; I've bathed. Better use that jar
of oil first; your shoulders look ugly. Is that armour-chafe,
or the heat? They may be blistered. Don't skimp with that oil
or you'll regret it tomorrow. He had good shoulders on Him,
didn't He? Good forearms, too. That surprised me. I'd never
have guessed Him powerfully built till they stripped. . . .

"Who? Did you ask who I'm talking about? By all the
leprous gods above us, do you mean anyone could have been
out there today and be thinking of anyone else, anything else?
—Oh, but of course. I've told myself every third minute since
that it was just a routine execution. That it was no different
from the hundred such I've watched, the score or more I've
been in charge of. If it didn't impress these Jews, why should
it have bothered a battle-scarred old Roman?

"And it didn't bother them. Those pigs walked all the way
out there just to watch Him die; they're at home now stuffing
themselves on the greasy leftovers from their feast, lecturing
their sons and daughters on the good life and jawing at their

wives because the storm muddied their holiday clothes; they'll sleep the sleep of the righteous tonight.

"And those few friends of His—did you notice how they came as close to the foot of His cross as I'd let them come? Didn't you notice the look on their faces? I couldn't decide which was worse to watch, them or Him. Those few friends will weep tonight. But what are tears in this world? Salt and water. They come easy and they dry easy, even easier than blood. They'll recover and forget, and go their way.

"Where's our Governor, now? Why, he's at dinner. Good appetite, Pilate! Where are the priests? Counting their money. Count it in good health, priests! It's 'business as usual' in beautiful Jerusalem.

"Why should I be the only madman in this whole rabbit-warren of a city, fool enough to feel that something went on out there today that isn't over, that's going to have some kind of sequel, that we were dealing with someone our Roman arms aren't long enough to reach, that when He lifted His face and looked into that storm and. . . .

"Varro—you're still young in the legion, in spite of your rank. You served first on the northern frontier against the Germans, didn't you? Do the veterans still worry fresh recruits with their warning, *'Never stare into the face of a man you've killed, or he'll come back in dreams to haunt you'?* There's a curse I wish would work! I'd be glad to see Him again, even in a dream.

"Oh, go ahead and dress, boy; quit watching me so owl-eyed! I've had no sunstroke, and I won't start wandering through the garrison mumbling these unmilitary fancies. It's just that I've bottled it up inside me all day and I've got to talk it out with someone. With all the officers brought into the city this week, why would I have drawn that execution?

"I've seen Him before, Varro—that Jesus. Must have been

three, maybe four years ago; I wasn't fifty yet. I was regional centurion up north at a town called Capernaum; it's His home country. I was there to keep order and enlist auxiliaries. That's a joke. Precious few enlistments there are up there! Well, this Man was causing such a stir and drawing such crowds that we had to keep an eye on Him. He was the sensation of the countryside, for a while.

"But it didn't take me long to see He was no rabble-rouser, no patriotic troublemaker of the sort we were there to look out for. What? No, no. He was a Teacher, and a Healer. Yes, He was. I tell you I watched Him! Often. Remember, Varro, how the myths they taught us as children back home described Apollo, the healing god, when he took on human form? We called this Man the Apollo of Galilee. My men laughed about it, but they stopped laughing when my orderly was so sick and I went to this Jesus—oh, never mind, you'd never believe it. Some who were there didn't believe it. But they stopped laughing.

"You'd better hurry if you're slated to eat at the first mess. What? What did He teach? Don't be a fool, I'm no scribe. But it's a bloody pity there were no scribes on His side, to get what He said written down somewhere so you could read it and think about it. But I'll tell you this, when you stood listening to Him in some hushed crowd, you weren't a Roman sneering, or a Jew snarling, or a Greek glaring or a slave cowering. The whole crowd of you belonged to something together, somehow, and you knew no matter what a fool you'd been with your life, it was worth changing. You knew you had played by the wrong rules, but that there were right rules now and it wasn't too late to try them. And oddest of all you knew that someone big, Varro, some power so big you were afraid to name it, knew all about you and yet was all for you, was counting on you and willing to help you.

"That *is* while you were there, while you were listening to Him. The magic went away somehow when you were out of the sound of His voice, out of sight of His face. Then life still seemed to be what it had been all along, an alley where the big dog gets the bone until the mad dog comes along.

"I had almost forgotten the spell He cast; I hadn't seen Him since my transfer, of course, until they brought Him in this morning. I had heard they were going to; they've been hatching this for weeks, just waiting for the right time. That near riot on Sunday clinched it. He was getting too big for them.

"You can't imagine what a rat I felt like this morning, when they placed Him under our arrest. I was terrified for fear He'd recognize me and show it, and let others know it. What a spot that would have put me in! *And I'm certain He did remember me.* But not a sign from Him. I tell you He knew it would embarrass me. What kind of a Man would care at that point whether He got someone else in trouble?

"But I got over that soon enough, at the flogging they gave Him! By Pollux, Varro, I'll get Sergeant Proclus for that somehow, the way that big lout handled that whip, more like a barbarian than a Roman. Did you ever see anyone take that kind of beating the way He did? I kept hoping He'd die under that flogging. I've seen men do it and spare themselves what followed. But not that One.

"*Whap!* would go that whip! *Whap!* it would go, and every time it cut home He'd go to His knees. When old Proclus would pause to get his breath, Jesus would shake the blood off His eyes and turn to see if Proclus were through. But never a tear, never a glare, never a curse. I got the queer notion He was wondering how many others Proclus had done that to. All through it, all through the trials and the mockery and the indignities, *He was more concerned with what we were doing to ourselves than with what was happening to Him!*

"But it was not until we got the order, and started—out there, pushing our way through the streets out to that miserable little hill—only then did I get this feeling I haven't been able to shake, that this was not my execution squadron and not yours, that Someone else was in command, that we weren't dragging Him up that hill, that staggering and stumbling as He did, *He was leading us:* that we didn't even set the stage out there, that if it had been in Greece or Rome or Egypt it still would have happened, *because something like it had to happen, and to Him!*

"He was in command as surely as if He had driven those nails Himself, and crimped them just as carefully as we did so that the hands couldn't tear loose even if the bones broke. He even helped us hoist it into place, even though He had crawled up unto its arms as if it were some throne He was to rule from.

"Didn't you see it, Varro? Didn't you feel something in the very air of the place? Did you have eyes only for the dice you threw and ears only for the taunts and jibes of that morbid crowd? Didn't you hear Him when He talked to Someone above Him there, as the clouds rushed in? Didn't you feel that Someone was listening? When the storm did break and the crowd scattered and that gloom came down as if heaven had dropped some terrible curtain, and that wind began to howl, I thought that cross silhouetted there against the lightning would soar on its outstretched arms like wings.

"When I felt the ground rock under our feet as if the thunder were crashing beneath us too, I meant it when I cried into the wind, *"Surely this was the Son of God."* I only hope He heard in time, I only hope He heard—what? Oh yes, you will be late. I'm sorry if I've kept you. No, no I'll be down for the second serving. And don't worry about me, boy, don't worry about me! I'm all right. . . .

"Why, the sun has gone down since I've been ranting. How dark it seems over Jerusalem. Wonder if it will ever be as bright again as it was this morning? Wonder where they took Him? Or—wonder if whoever was listening above Him out there was waiting to welcome . . . but why not a prayer? To Jesus Apollo? Doesn't fit. That man was no myth. Why not Jesus Caesar? Imperial Jesus. That fits! That fits! *Jesus Caesar, wherever you are, you heard a Roman's salute today. Now hear a Roman's prayer. I have looked into the face of One I killed. Now come back and haunt me. Come back and haunt me until I understand what I only dimly felt our there today!*"

". . . You know that I've never been willing to make the leap of faith, and now I can find no reason for wanting to. . . . I suppose the truth is I'm so placidly, busily happy that I can't honestly imagine that life won't go on and on, the way it is right now."

—*A Girl We'll Call Jean*

9

THE SAINTS OF GOD ANONYMOUS

LET'S CALL HER Jean, though none of you know her. Her letter pleased me, intrigued me and distressed me, all at the same time and on different levels. It's always good to hear unexpectedly from a friend, and it's always intriguing to try to trace just what it is that keeps an agnostic determined to go on being an agnostic. But it's always distressing if this agnostic is someone you admire, and for whom you want the best. For the life of determined doubt, no matter how attractively it's packaged, is far from the best, and it does not wear well across the years in the twists and frictions of living.

I haven't seen this girl for some years now. But I remember her home where she grew up, brighter than most of us—or should I say more sensitive than most of us? I hardly know which term to use, for they both may mean the same thing. There was an intensity about her which I realize now meant among other things that she was trying harder than the rest of us to grope her way between the opposite religious views on which her parents clashed.

During her college years she regretfully pronounced the

last rites over whatever faith she had kept. I'm rather certain I could even name the college professor, a professor of religion, who officiated at that burial of faith. In the name of an enlightened religion he taught her all of the logic of doubt but none of the reasons for belief. He was one of those tweedy, affable cynics, all charm on the campus or at a faculty tea, who can smile and quip in three languages and arch an eyebrow boyishly and tell you everything that's wrong with your church and your religious background, but who somehow never get around to anything that's right, or hopeful, or strong, or abiding. You know the type: all scholar for the board of trustees where it counts, all razor in the classroom where it hurts.

Oh, no one made a cynic out of Jean. Not her home, not her school. That's what was so striking. She was the sort of person who seemed to be a walking advertisement against religion, thoroughly agnostic, yet fine and kind and good. She was convinced that there really isn't anything in life to hang on to, yet she had a gift of fondness for people, and a quiet determination to be as happy as one can be with what one has while here, and to share that courage and determination with others.

She's happily married now, and a useful, admirable young citizen. That's exactly what she wrote me about—how happy she is without what I was always trying to urge on her. She wrote, "You know that I've never been willing to make the leap of faith, and now I can find no reason for wanting to. Perhaps I'll be sorry some day, when I'm really rocked with trouble. But of course I must slip in the reminder that we who have no God have been known to stand up to trouble too! I suppose the truth is I'm so placidly, busily happy that I can't honestly imagine that life won't go on and on, the way it is right now!"

What sense are you and I supposed to make of that kind of person? I don't know too many like her, but I know enough like her, and so do you, that they demand some notice. We're forever insisting in the church that the mystery of life requires God to explain it and to enable us to cope with it, that a human being must have his standard of conduct rooted in a faith that gives it meaning and support. But there's Jean, and there are those you could name, who manage well enough without God, it would seem, who get along not only happily enough but quite admirably, if you please, without God.

Or so they think. And that's our clue, that "so they think." They think they're having nothing to do with God but that's humanly impossible. While reading Jean's letter, I thought of a prominent New York clergyman telling how he walked the streets of one of our great cities one night with a man terribly disturbed because he could not believe. This was a man of deep humane sympathies and great ability and wide achievement for good who wished he could accept God, but somehow couldn't. As they walked there where the street crowds thinned and the glare of lights dimmed and the city noises faded to a constant but muted roar, he kept comparing his friend with people he knew who did believe in God because they had been brought up to believe in God, and had never faced the tears and misery of things sympathetically enough to have their faith shaken.

He kept comparing them with this doubter, this fine-grained doubter who, because of his very love for people, his sense of justice, his resentment of the "sufferings that fall with such terrific incidence upon the vast, obscure forgotten masses of mankind," kept turning at every stoplight to ask, "How can you believe a good God made a world like this?" After they had talked it over for hours on the sidewalks of the city, the clergyman shook his friend's hand and quoted to him these words from Isaiah, "[And God said to Cyrus], *I girded thee, though thou hast not known me.*"

That's an astonishing thing to find in the Bible, for if ever there was a pagan who had nothing to do with the God of the Bible, it was Cyrus, the King of the Medes and Persians. He was a crass idolator, a worshiper of the fierce dark gods, Bel and Nebo. But here he was, the hope of the hour. Here he was about to destroy Babylon, the monstrous city, and free all the ancient East from the terrors of its dominance. He was about to free the exiles of Israel from their long captivity, and send them home to rebuild the walls and the temple of Jerusalem. As he appeared on time's stage as a champion, a liberator, the very instrument of God Himself, the faithful of Israel were puzzled, even as their hopes soared. How can this be, they asked among themselves, how can God work through this pagan? How can undeniable good come from this godless man?

Isaiah, the prophet in exile, answers them; "Don't you know that God can use any man to praise Him? Can't you hear the Almighty saying to Cyrus, *I girded thee, though thou hast not known me?* I have created you and strengthened you, empowered you and used you, even though you haven't any notion who I am"? Moffat translates these words, *"[Cyrus], you know me not, but I delight in you."* If you and I will give that our hand and let it lead us for a quiet stroll up the lane of its meaning, we'll never let anyone bother us again by pointing to high-minded, admirable people who do not recognize God, and who use their lives as an argument against God.

You won't find too many of them. They are the exception rather than the rule. But when you do see them, recognize them for what they are. *They are Saints of God Anonymous.* That's what Jean is, who wrote me this letter, though I can fairly hear her laughter at the title. That's what that man was with whom that minister walked the city streets that night.

What they bear witness to is the tremendous fact that the God and Father of Jesus Christ can't be defined or pigeonholed by our limited ideas as to the way He works.

God doesn't stand around idly shifting from one foot to the other, waiting helplessly to be recognized or received before He can do anything with or for a human life. He is an unavoidable fact, and we can no more refuse to have personal dealings with Him, recognized or not, than we can manage to live in the physical world and refuse to have dealings with the facts and forces of nature.

After all, this isn't so unheard of when you think of it—our being helped, strengthened, lifted, used by forces of which we're unaware, or which we simply do not understand. Through so many centuries mankind had only the most fantastic misconceptions of nature, and saw the world around him through the eyes of childish or grotesque myth and ignorance. Yet through all those centuries the sunshine which man didn't understand proceeded to warm him. The rain he could neither predict nor explain brought his harvests and refreshed him. He didn't know what to make of the return of spring, why it should happen again and again, but it meant life to him. Of the stars and the planets he knew least of all, yet they steered his boats and lifted his thoughts, and that enigmatic moon meant romance long before we could measure its craters or time an eclipse. Would you say that until a child understands his father and mother they can do nothing for him and mean nothing to him? It's quite an exercise in humility to begin the listing of forces and factors to which we've been indebted and by which we've been richly blessed long before we were aware of them enough so much as to call them by name.

Let's write this down in whatever color ink we use when we want something underlined indelibly: *our religion can't begin to take the measure of life until we open it to the sweeping realization that this God we worship is the source of all good, no matter what name it uses or where it is found.* God is wherever the spirit of mankind flowers into strengths and beauties mere beasts could never know; wherever men light up the night around them by the lift of sacrificial loyalties, or that sustained tenderness which is the very opposite of weakness, or that compassion which asks no favors but to be true to its own outgoing sympathy, or that devotion to the best which would rather hurt with the right than prosper with the wrong: wherever we see such goodness in people, whether they recognize its source or not, a Christian should be the first to acknowledge it and be glad, *knowing that there walks God,* that slipping through some door left ajar, He has been at work in that life, and even though He's had to work incognito, He delights in the results. Let that be our first thought with any such we know, to remember to say what L. P. Jacks said of a friend, "Look at him; isn't he an inspiration? He spends his breath arguing that there is no God, but spends his life proving that there is!" That first, before the afterthought occurs, as it also should to a Christian, "But isn't it a shame that he won't recognize who it is has had such rewarding dealing with him?"

One of my most embarrassing hours came to me as a would-be high-school dramatist. Our drama teacher, woefully short of talent, was forced to cast me in roles for which nature simply had not fashioned me. The worst was the role of the starving convict in the play *The Bishop's Candlesticks,* where my entrance line was a hoarse-voiced announcement that I had not eaten in five days! At 230 pounds this convulsed the crowd so violently I don't think they heard another line of the drama. I doubt if the footlights have ever disclosed a starving convict so round, so firm, so fully-packed.

And equally futile were my efforts in the title role of the play, *Daddy Long Legs,* especially in the sequence where the light from an open door was supposed to cast my shadow long, tall and thin across the stage. My shadow just wouldn't stretch, somehow, and what was meant to be a tender, haunting scene again broke up the house. But surely many of you remember that play by Jean Webster, performed by somewhat more credible casts, written back when the American stage didn't believe that in order to be wise it had to be morbid and complex and savage, when we dared to be obvious and forthright and hopeful. It was the story of the girl in an orphanage befriended by a man who kept his identity unknown. A young bachelor, he was so charmed by the homeless girl that across the years he maintained for her a silent sponsorship. Only once had she seen his shadow cast from an open office door, and she thought of him in terms of that shadow. And even though she actually met him often in person, she didn't recognize him as her benefactor. On through to maturity her every favor and opportunity came her way through this anonymous friend. Of course the play had a happy ending: a final scene when she discovers who he is. It's when that scene is missing that the romance strangely resembles tragedy in people whose lives have been sponsored, whose hearts have been nurtured, whose mistakes have been buttressed and whose achievements have been shaped by Someone in the shadow who has no name to them.

Of course I doubt if I'll quote anything that obvious when I answer Jean's letter, but I may say this: C. S. Lewis insists that our biggest surprise when we see God is that He will not look strange to us. We'll have no faintest conception till that very hour how He will look, but when we see Him we'll know we've always known Him, and we'll realize with a start what part He has played at many an hour in our lives when we have thought ourselves alone. That fleeting sense we've often had of Someone friendly nearby will be explained. That central music that sings through every moment of happiness, and then evades our memory, will be recovered, for we won't say to God, when we see Him, "Who are you?" We'll say, "So it was You all the time!" I may quote that to Jean.

By the way, while we've been talking about Jean, could we—could we by any chance have been talking to you?

". . . I guess that's the trouble with machines; you still must have people to run them. And there's no guarantee comes with the machines as to what kind of people you'll get!"

The Chocolate-Dipper

10

THAT'S THE TROUBLE WITH HORSES

I HEARD LAST summer the strange lament of a chocolate-dipper.
I had never met a chocolate-dipper before, at least not know-
ingly. I was alone at a table in the diner of the train from
Buffalo. Let me hurry to admit that when this young lady took
the chair across from mine it was hardly a tribute to me; all
the other seats were taken. But let it also be recorded that
she didn't hesitate, for she was a rather large young lady, and
I've noticed that there's always a certain free masonry among
large people. We seem to sense a potential kindred soul in
anyone who so obviously is carrying our same burden. As I
remember, rather early in our routine exchange of those
lurching pleasantries that are the code on diners, the information was volunteered that she was by career a chocolate-
dipper—and a good one, if she did say so herself! This was
offered, I noticed, without particular enthusiasm. I assured
her that though I knew very little about the candy industry
I feared that in my brief span I had done more than one man's
share in providing it a market, and how were things going in
the world of chocolate-dipping at the moment?

This was her answer, this homely little American version of a business success that was not quite humanly successful. Things were going swimmingly in the world of chocolate-dipping. Her family long had owned a candy concern in Ohio. Business was, if anything, too good. "But," she said—and how often have you heard these same accents in other circumstances—"the candy business isn't much fun any more. We thought when we got those machines that all our troubles would be over, for you do well to dip by hand a hundred and fifty pounds a day. We have machines now that turn out two thousand pounds a day. All I do is supervise the girls who run those machines. Our plant has grown unbelievably. We have everything we had worked for. I don't know why we shouldn't be on top of the world." Then, as she poked disconsolately with her fork at the railroad's tortured notion of Salisbury steak, she said this in so offhand a manner that I know she couldn't have sensed how wise it was. *"I guess that's the trouble with machines; you still must have people to run them. And there's no guarantee comes with the machines as to what kind of people you'll get!"*

Back in my chair car I didn't even try to finish the book I had started; just stared out the window, much to the annoyance I'm certain of the chatty lady across the aisle, who probably told her niece in Youngstown that what's wrong with the church today is how rude and aloof ministers can get just as you think you're getting acquainted with them. But you don't get that kind of meat served often with Salisbury steak! *"That's the trouble with machines; you still must have people to run them!"* I can't retrace the back passageways of the mind that led me across thousands of years to an old scene of battle, and to the taunt a pagan soldier hurled at Jerusalem before that city fell. The Assyrian army had surrounded Jerusalem. There was no way of escape from these Nazis of the

ancient East. The citizens within the city were demoralized
and ready to surrender, but Hezekiah, the King of Jerusalem,
was trusting to Egypt to get him out of trouble. He had an
agreement with the Pharaoh that Egypt would furnish him
arms, would send him the famed Egyptian chariots and horses
with which to fight. No army could stand against those horses.
The Assyrian commander stands outside the walls this day
and calls a taunt to the guards in the towers, a message you
can loosely phrase this way: "Go tell the King of Jerusalem
he's a fool. Go tell him he's through. Go tell him he's putting
his trust for deliverance in something that is not strength.
You'll find him standing now at his palace window scanning
the southern horizon, staring down toward Edom, watching
the plains of Moab for the first dim swirl of that cloud of
dust which will mean his friend, the Pharaoh, has delivered,
that here come the horses! Hasn't your King forgotten something? What good are horses? We'll gladly do the same for
him. I swear my King will drive through your gates two thous-
and horses, if you can put riders on their backs, able and loyal
men! Go tell the King of Jerusalem that *that's the trouble with
horses. You still must have men to ride them, and there's no
guarantee comes with the horses as to what kind of riders
you'll get!"*

The odd lament of a chocolate-dipper, the scornful taunt
of an ancient commander, and in between them three thous-
and years of human experience. Still, it's news! Still, the lesson
is never quite learned, and the clicking roar of the wheels on
the track of a train from Buffalo seemed to be saying over and
over, "That's the trouble, that's the trouble. *Whether it's horses
or machines, we're forever expecting a well-equipped life to be
an automatically happy life. We're forever assuming that if
we have great means by which to live, that will insure great
aims for which to live. We're forever trusting that victory in*

any venture is guaranteed simply by having at our disposal enough of the paraphernalia and devices and stage props of our world."

All human history is one great rambling footnote to that mistake. What good are horses, what good are machines, unless you've a certain quality of person to ride them or run them? The best of equipment means nothing but more complicated trouble, unless it is used by a brand of men and women mere equipment can never produce: men and women who, no matter what their equipment, would still have the intangibles of a faith in God worth living by, a wholeness of heart worth living with, and loyalty to causes worth living for!

It takes a certain stubborn courage today to be platitudinal, to beat the drums for the commonplace, for there aren't any means by which the Christian tradition can make this particular truth fresh and exciting. There isn't a pew in any church where we could get real argument on this theme, at least not in theory. For this has been so steadily the voice of religion, these are so obviously the accents of Christ, that anyone who has spent any time even within hailing distance of a church has heard it a thousand times. But that's exactly why our church, our faith is so desperately eager today that we resell this commonplace to ourselves, heat up this platitude until it burns our minds a little, singes into our thinking. *We American Christians keep on talking as if it were true but living as if it were not.* Mentally we may vote a cautious "yes" to it, but emotionally we go on expecting the horses to save us, expecting machines to solve it for us, trusting naïvely that the better the equipment the better the life. You cannot name any single foolishness that has done us more harm, that has gone further in producing the most terrifying fact of the present— jet-propelled ape, the moral moron at the controls, the cave man in the Cadillac!

Look over your shoulder for just one glance, as Lloyd Morris did in his haunting volume of American memories, *Postscript to Yesterday*. Rake the leaves of our history back there in the 1890's, and you catch a whiff of the atmosphere of boundless optimism. Today was good and tomorrow would be better. Optimism was as natural and American as the wide verandahs and the metal stag that guarded the lawn, the gas-lit parlor and the social call with card and kid gloves, sarsaparilla and mandolins and the tandem bike and the family outing, or the sherbet served with the roast when company came for dinner after church! It was as much a part of the scene as all that to assume that our horizons were un-limited, that we could take for granted a large, cheerful aver-age of health and success and exuberant living, that we might argue a little as to how, but there was nothing wrong in our world that our collective ability and ingenuity could not make right. It was a queer fish back there who could remain a pessimist.

Then turn around and look around, and it's a different uni-verse. Oh, progress unlimited all right, in externals. In fifty, sixty years all these unbelievable physical and social miracles, this breathless advance, as had no other nation in history, in power and wealth and possessions; these, we kept saying, couldn't fail to keep life happy and secure. And these stagger-ing, heady, intoxicating conquests of the good earth and sea and sky—where everything from steam to the very air's im-palpable variations, from the lightning to the secret creation had locked inside the atom, from vapors to the mould that eats the bread crust—everything was harnessed to empower or heal or comfort or amuse us. But in this matter of morale, what was this warm and wonderful something that had vanished, leaving hardly a memory? As our standard of living has gone steadily up our level of confidence has dipped steadily down.

Here we are as a people at the peak of our powers. Then why has trust evaporated? Why should America have found itself hated most by some of its most gifted youth as no great nation has ever been before? Why in these years should visitors from abroad find with astonishment fears and suspicions and distrust more extreme than those prevailing in war-wrecked Europe? Why did the dream at the moment of fruition begin to wisp away into mirage? Why has the American weather of faith-in-itself turned with each victory from fair to stormy? Where are the happiness and security we had guaranteed ourselves? Why would they tell you, and they will tell you, *"It is a queer fish today who can remain an optimist"*? Could it be possible that what an Englishman—of all people! and a clergyman at that, the late Archbishop William Temple—had been warning us of for years was true? "You're the best hope of earth," he said, "but you're letting yourself be duped and cheated and taken in by trusting something that in the long haul cannot deliver." Here are the horses. But what about the riders? Here are those great, big wonderful machines. But what about the people who run them? That's the trouble, that's always the trouble!

We can't dodge it again in our lifetime, you see. Everywhere we turn, it's facing us. On every road we travel it meets us. Every door we start to knock on, it taps our shoulder first. It's the question mark all over America just as it is in our own Greater Pittsburgh. Who could fail to be thrilled and amazed as he watches the Triangle become that gleaming symbol of industrial power, studded with soaring monuments to man's ingenuity, as he walks among unbelievable shafts of steel or aluminum, along what has become in every truth the Boulevard of the Alloys! You try to measure the power all this represents and you can't; you can only sense it, and you think of that word Carlyle coined once, the word "gigantesque"! But when this autumn breeze surges, its fresh whisper is an old challenge from the Voice of History which wise men call God, saying to a city, "I'll give you horses. Can you put the riders on their backs? I gave the horses to Babylon; you'd have thrilled to the power of Babylon. But the hot wind from the Persian Gulf can't find its walls and turrets now, and the sober scholars sift the sands and argue, 'Where was Babylon?' I sent horses to Carthage. What a power was Carthage! But the jungle has reclaimed its streets, and the jackal laughs where once they schemed dominion, and the guide who tells you he knows where Hannibal's palace stood, lies. I sent horses to Rome, and to so many a Rome since. But the Coliseum looks bleached, like the bones of some unburied monster, and the seed of the Caesars beg from tourists along the drabness that was once the Appian Way. I've sent you the horses, never before in such number. This could be the last delivery. Can you put riders on their backs?"

America won't even hear that question until we do. And God knows America won't answer, won't know how or what to answer, until you and I quit playing around with religion. For Christianity is no mere religion. It's the truth about life. It's a certain way of dealing with life because that's the only way life will work, because Almighty God is exactly like Jesus Christ! Aren't we ready, aren't we finally ready to let that God do big business with you and me at last?

Said the student, "I suppose I'm supposed to be a Christian."

"Now isn't that amazing!" concluded the Bishop. . . .

11

THAT'S YOUR QUESTION

THE CHAPLAIN of the University of Edinburgh told me about it. The speaker at the chapel that morning had been an Englishman, born in India, and now one of the younger bishops of the Christian Church in India. The students had been invited to remain after the service if they cared to question the speaker and one student had challenged the speaker in accents anyone who has spent any time on a modern college campus will recognize, in that weird jumble of bright eyes and dirty white buck shoes, straight-A students and split-T quarterbacks. This student had said to the speaker quite angrily, "I didn't expect to hear this provincial and narrow message from you, of all people! You've seen so much of our world. You've looked at the twentieth century from so many corners of the room. Yet all you talked about was Christ. All you seem to have to say to us is something about Christ. Why Christ? Why didn't you bring us some insight from Mohammed? Why didn't you bring us some inspiration from Buddha? Wouldn't that have been just as valid?"

The speaker looked at him with a disarming smile and said

quietly, "Oh, are you a Moslem?" "Why, no," answered the lad. "Then," said the Bishop, "just as I thought, Mohammed is not your problem. Are you a Buddhist?" "Of course not," snapped the boy. "Then I was right. Buddha is not your problem. What are you then?" "Why, I don't know," the student shifted uncomfortably, because this wasn't coming out at all the way he had planned, *"I suppose I'm supposed to be a Christian!"* "Now isn't that amazing!" concluded the Bishop, "I've never had that vague an answer from a Moslem. I've never had that vague an answer from a Buddhist. And I've lived and have dealt with them all my life. You know, if I were you I wouldn't worry myself too much about their faith, until I have made up my own mind about Jesus Christ. *Because it's easy to see He's your problem!"*

That dialogue doesn't seem at all collegiate or alien, does it? Doesn't it suggest how a good many things that bother a good many of us can fall into rough but usable shape? Ever since *Life* magazine, well over a year ago, began its series on the Great Religions of Mankind I've had people saying to me, "By the way, the Moslem religion is quite a faith isn't it?" or "Say, I didn't realize how much there is to Buddhism," and saying it in an almost furtive manner, as if this were guilty knowledge they had come by, and perhaps it would be better if it weren't noised about, since it seemed somehow embarrassing to our Christian claims.

Let's say it now and as often as it needs saying: *It is no secret that God has always been at work in all the great religions of mankind.* This has been no news to Christianity since St. Paul first insisted on it, and he did insist on it! All the great religions can be seen as God's attempt to get through to man, in every age, in every land. But it also is no secret that Christianity claims that *only in the Man from Nazareth did God really get through, really arrive in Person!*

You protest, "Wait a minute! First you're saying there's some truth of God in other faiths that must be respected. Then in the next breath you're saying Christ is the *Big* Truth, the *Full* Truth about God! How can you hold to both of those statements at once? How can you underscore the one without shortchanging the other?" That's the puzzle.

Of course it is. Of course it puzzles you. It puzzles me. It puzzles anyone who has ever given brief or disciplined thought to the matter. Don't ever expect to find any weight or reasoning that's heavy and hot enough to iron out and smooth away that wrinkle in our thinking. It's another place where the man of faith must be willing cheerfully and unashamedly to say, "I don't know!"

I was a guest at a Jewish Temple. I had been invited to lecture on "What a Christian Believes About Christ." After the hour there were questions for over an hour, probing questions in an atmosphere you could feel was charged by the attempt of those people to imagine what possible shape a faith could take that actually maintained that the Eternal, whom Moses dared not look upon, had walked on feet like our feet and reached with hands like our hands, and died a death like our death, that we might in some fragmentary fashion live a life like His life.

And at the close of the evening their Rabbi took my breath by quoting an ancient rabbinical admonition. "Remember, my people," he said to them, "remember as you go your way that in some fashion we cannot understand, *the words this man teaches and the words I teach are both the words of the Living God!*" I went home in a turmoil, thinking, "How could he say that?" We didn't agree, he and I. Wasn't one of us dead right and the other dead wrong? Hadn't I made claims for Christ that were either true or false? Hadn't they rejected those claims either to their own credit or their own hurt? Then

how could there be any sense in saying this haunting thing
that both of us in some fashion spoke the words of the Living
God?

But you see, that is not my problem. If that is true in some
fashion I cannot understand, how it can be true is not my
problem, any more than it is my problem, as Dr. Paul Scherer
says somewhere, how Vega, that blue star which sat squarely
up over my head of a night this summer and seemed to sit up
there on nothing at all, and weighs God only knows how
much, how it can be true that such a monster swims into my
night sky and all in orderly fashion winks at me its blue pin
point of light from such an incredible distance away. That puzzles me. I wonder at it. But it is not my problem to justify it.
I just know it's there. *And it is not my task to reconcile the
claim Jesus Christ has made on my life with the view of Him
that is taken by those on whom He has made no claim.* Putting
aside for the moment all the things I don't know and con-
centrating on the things I do know, even if like the lad at
school I only "suppose I'm supposed to be a Christian"—well,
what do I make of Christ? *He's* my problem. *That's* my question.

Jesus Himself sharpened the focus of that question. It was
as far from home as we have any record of Christ's journeying,
far to the north of Galilee, far for men who had walked all the
way, and camped at night under the trees, where the wild
figs could vary the fare of the bread they had brought or
begged on the way. There at the nothern limits of Palestine
where broad Mt. Hermon stands guard, and from the foothills that seem to be the mountains' own gnarled roots, the
melting snow sends down the rivulets that form the Jordan
River and begin its flow to the south. Up there on some un-
claimed terrace of the foothills where the air had a mountain
freshness to it, and the dust of the southern plains yielded to

the scent of oleander, where even penniless fishermen from Galilee could find relief from the late summer heat, and an unemployed Carpenter could camp out with His friends and escape the press of the crowds in the villages and gather spent strength for His last campaign, His own kind of march toward Jerusalem, there in camp one day He startled them by asking suddenly, "You've talked to people about Me. What do they make of Me? Who are they saying I am?"

"Oh," is the answer from several as they turn to listen, sensing the urgency in His voice, "they don't—people don't know quite what to make of you. There's every shape of rumor. Many insist you must be John the Baptist come alive again. And others urge, no, He's another Elijah. Still others call you a returned Jeremiah. Each seems to find in you his favorite prophet."

By now the disciples are huddled around waiting—what a chance this is to evaluate all these strange and lively rumors! *"But who do you say that I am?"* The question came like a suddenly pointed finger, with all that individualizing genius of Christ's. Their main task was not to sort and compare every shade and slant of village rumor. No matter what men who had heard Him once or twice, had seen Him now and then, might think of Jesus, what did these friends of His think about Him? These men into whose lives He had walked, whose whole current of life He had rechannelled, whose minds He had sharpened, whose loyalties He had mastered, whose hopes He had fired—no matter what the rest of the world might think or say about Him, what had they, on the basis of what they had seen and known, what had *they* decided about Him? *That was their question. And it's your question too.*

Because His claim has been made on us. That's the trouble when you and I try to get by even for a season on just "supposing we're supposed to be Christians." Something in us knows there should be so much more to it than that. Some depth in us has at some time responded to some height it has ever been voiced—that this Man, who moved through hunger in us has sampled His fulfillment, and though we feed it to pacify it with every other saccharine substitute, that part of us dimly knows it's hungry still and it's going to go on being either Christ-healed or Christ-haunted.

Because He is in our midst. He is among us, and He has been here for a long, long time. Those sandals we think of Him as wearing wouldn't last long on our streets. That mantle we always picture Him in would be unthinkably thin to hold off our winters. As we glance our world's way, we wonder just where He would fit in. But you see, He didn't fit in back there either. There wasn't any place for Him back there. They made His life as hard as nails in His shop or the nails in His cross. His family looked on Him as demented and virtually disowned Him. His church branded Him as a blasphemer and excommunicated Him. His country tried Him as a traitor and crucified Him. His friends decided He was a starry-eyed bungling failure and deserted Him. That's what you'd call being squeezed out of your world with a vengeance, isn't it?

And yet He made it. He got into lives. He got into minds and hearts and wills. He got in so deeply that before the world could believe its ears it was hearing the strangest claim that has ever been voiced—that this Man, who moved through all the lights and shadows that we know and yet made of the very shadows themselves another glory, this man, who feared nothing but fear and hated nothing but hatred and proved love to be not an indulgence but a power, and mercy to be not a weakness, but a force, that this was no one other than the Eternal focused in time, the truth about man as man should live by the power of God, and the truth about God so far as God could live before the eyes of man!

You and I, seldom worse yet seldom better than all the others back up the years, have hidden and obscured Him and His own church quite as often as we've proclaimed Him. The drift of our lives has denied His Lordship far oftener than it has affirmed it. And yet, don't doubt for a moment that His hallmark is on us. He has invaded our thinking too, and channelled our compassion. He gleams in even our clumsier attempts at brotherhood. He has put a mold to our eternal hopes that all our despair and doubting can't quite twist entirely out of shape. And all of this when we're often least aware of it.

The loose-lipped man can't even swear without calling Him by name. The atheist can't date a letter without witnessing His birth. Every time a warning hand is placed on today's thirst for power and immensities, and something warns, "What will it profit to gain all this yet lose our souls?"—that's Christ talking. Every time one of us suffers yet forgets himself and by that self-forgetfulness adds to mankind's slender margin of patience and courage and overcoming love—there's Christ at work. We're Christians in the rough, in the raw, in more ways than we ever dream.

Then why isn't it more obvious, more concerted, more apparent? If Christ is in our midst, even though gone underground so often, why doesn't the Christian Church accomplish more, stand for more, achieve more? But, you know, that isn't your question! Your question involves you. Your question is, "Now that it's gone on this long, now that He's been with us this long, what do you really believe about, how do you honestly feel toward, what do you actually do because of Jesus whom men call the Christ?"

"You know, that's the trouble with religion. You take old Governor Campbell. There he is stiff as a billy goat again. But if a revival hits town this winter, you know who'll be converted first!"

—*The Man in the Barber Shop*

12

CONVERTED AT EVERY REVIVAL

OLD GOVERNOR CAMPBELL was undisputed chief of the village bums in our home town. Remarkably little was known about him for a town that tried to know all the unfortunate facts about everyone in sight, and to make it the first order of business never to forget, and never to let the victim of its memory forget that it remembered. But old Governor Campbell was simply there, as much a part of the scenery as the Court House or the Clayton Building, between which he shuffled and in front of which he sunned: on the Court House lawn of a morning, on the curb in the shade of an afternoon.

None of us ever thought to ask, so far as I can remember, when he had drifted into town. What sequence of moral traps had he been caught in across a lifetime to reduce him to this shiftless, shameless old derelict? Which village wit had first fastened on him that absurd, cruel title, "Governor"? What vestige of inverted pride dictated that he accept and use the name as a tribute rather than a jibe? He had outlived those who knew the answers to these, and the rest of us never thought to ask.

I can't remember a time when he wasn't out on the street
in clear weather, greeting those merchants he knew with some
coarse, wily witticism, some one of the barbed vulgarities
which were his stock-in-trade, the barter with which he
sponged quarters from the lawyers as they would come from
the Court House. One quarter meant that he ate that day.
Two quarters meant he could get drunk for supper. If his
comments on the news or the weather sparked something you
could quote to the boys at lunch, the more solid citizens
thought it worth a quarter.

Since moss grows on memory too, you and I can find it
very easy to grow sentimental about the old home town.
Sharper memories might remind us that the old home town was
seldom sentimental about itself. I doubt if anyone ever looked
at Governor Campbell and wondered what a manhood must
have been his once for his body to take the punishment he
gave it daily, yearly, now! What ambitions had he known once?
What raw early powers of mind had been damped and stifled
down to the low, animal cunning he still retained? Was there
some spring which he, like other men, remembered above
all others, the touch of anyone in affection, the look of anyone
in respect? The quarters tossed him on the street didn't know
enough to ask such things. They meant neither charity nor
sympathy. They were frightened, nervous, superstitious quarters, tossed by men who knew human wreckage when they
saw it, and expected nothing but further wreckage ever to
come of it, and hoped instinctively that by the alchemy of
alms, the magic of a quick tip, they could keep such wreckage at a distance.

That's why he shocked them so when he would step out
of character. For, you see, old Governor Campbell was converted at every revival! The Southwest's own version of the
tent-meeting, the sawdust trail, a particularly bewildering

blend of sincerity and emotional extravagance, was still very much in vogue. And every year or so the Governor would be converted. The news would spread from the Court House to the barber shops: "I hear old Governor's got religion again." It would be told as a joke, with many a laugh. But it was a hollow joke. It was nervous laughter. For sure enough, there he'd be, clean-shaven, hair trimmed, his shabby clothes at least laundered and pressed, not lounging in some favorite corner but standing erect out on the street for a few days—never more than for a few days! You would see the press go out of his suit as the slouch came back into his shoulders. You could watch the stubble and grime come back on his chin as the proud little blue lights went out in his eyes. He would seem to wilt visibly under the brutal barrage from the curbstone wits, "How many days now, Guv'ner? Would you lead all us sinners in prayer, Guv'ner? Hear you're takin' up preachin' yourself, Guv'ner!"

That would do it. That would always do it. Long before the cool gusts of the autumn winds would come to send the dead leaves scuttling like crabs across the Court House lawn, he'd be back in character, and those who seemed to enjoy the spectacle would slip him a quarter and a knowing wink, and might say to their barber later, as he stropped his razor in a cadence that was meant to keep time with their wisdom, "You know, that's the trouble with religion. You take old Governor Campbell. There he is stiff as a billy goat again. But if a revival hits town this winter, you know who'll be converted first!"

How was I to know as I listened that these adults, who seemed so sure of themselves and what they were saying, were sure of neither and frightened of both? How would I have dared had I known enough—which I didn't—how would I have dared to say to them, "You're terribly mistaken. The trouble isn't with religion. You laugh at this old derelict when you're a major part of his tragedy. For you don't believe, and you won't let him believe that a man can be changed. His disaster isn't that he gets converted at every revival. His tragedy is much the same as ours; he simply doesn't get converted often enough."

It took me more than twenty years to feel the teeth of that village parable. Perhaps it has very little to do with tent-meetings and village tramps and unrecapturable yesterdays. But surely it has ever so much to do with you and me and the lives we're gearing from day to day now, and all that the suggestion of a new beginning, of making a fresh start, keeps whispering to our hearts in spite of our suspicions. We've missed something basic, something right at the roots of Christian living, if we've never realized how much Christianity consists of a whole lifetime of fresh starts. That's an ineluctable flare of its genius. That is so often why Christ can do so much with and for such unlikely material as we are, if we'll continue to let Him at our lives all our lives. Every high occasion, every milestone reached which persuades us to peer ahead and glance back and take a look around, every hour that demands we take honest inventory of the pattern our days have been weaving, certainly every time we come together for worship, was meant to be a revival. *And you and I are meant to be converted at every revival.*

How else would you sum up in brief the Biblical view of the meaning of life? Perhaps we shouldn't try to sum it up in brief. That may be one of our troubles—this passion we have for the short cut, the quickie gospel, the abridged version. There surely are some things too big to boil down. That may be why thumbnail sketches so often are only hangnail sketches. Frank Halliday Ferris has come up with a surprising double-thrust by way of just such a summary which may strike you as deceivingly simple. Only as you weigh it and feel of it and stare at it do you begin to realize how deep and how far it goes. He insists that the Bible from first to last takes as its constant comment and prophecy on any man that all our lives, every day of our lives so long as we are in this world, you and I will never be free from having trouble with ourselves. That truce is never signed. We never cease to be a walking civil war. To be human means there will be within us struggle, struggle, struggle, all the way. The only claim the Bible makes on which it is more insistent than that relentless prophecy is this magnificent confidence: If we mean gallant business with this struggle we will have resources beyond our own to draw upon, and an unfaltering Ally, undismayed, all-wise, merciful, who is even more eager for us to win than we are!

Isn't that the confidence from which Paul wrote Philippians? You can almost see him pause in this letter he's sending back to those friends in that church he loved above all others, pause and look up. His words have been flowing in that steady, powerful style of his, pumping red, warm, vital blood through the great themes of faith and hope and love. And it's as if suddenly the thought struck him with a new force—and what a consolation it has been to all the lesser preachers down the years that this thought should strike Paul too—"Why, here I am urging these achievements, advising these goals of living, and I haven't reached them myself! Wrong still attracts me. Pride and ambition and resentment still ambush me. This body I'm using still manages so often to get the upper hand and take me over. Every day it's a battle. Every day in so many ways it's much the same battle. And time and again I lose. I hope they won't think when they read this letter that I— but I must make that plain!" And he writes the surging words Christians have seized upon ever since as our Charter of Personal Renewal. "Don't think," he urges, "that I imagine for a moment that I've arrived in taking hold of that style of living for which the Christ has taken hold of me. But I go on trying because every day with me is a fresh start. *For this one thing I do. By the power of God's forgiveness I cut myself loose from the things I failed in yesterday. By the power of God's renewal I reach ahead eagerly to try it His way again tomorrow.*" He made his life a constant pattern of forever getting started again. Every time he gathered his scattered heart together before God He knew that could mean revival. And he was determined to be converted at every revival.

As surely as you need more of God in your life, some corner of that fits some dent in your heart right now. Only you and God know which corner and which dent. You know that there's some failure within you at the moment that you can't explain away, that you can't shift the blame for to anyone else. There's something you're tired of, afraid of, disgusted with, resentful about. There's some defeat you've suffered in the clash of rival ambitions within you, and no matter what you tell yourself about that defeat, it still rankles. Some slap in the face of your dreams has been dealt you by life's unexplainable restrictions, and no matter how you argue with yourself, the cheeks of your dreams still burn. Some ghost of unadmitted, unresolved guiltiness keeps playing hobgoblin to frighten both your ideals and your abilities, so that no matter how you urge them on, your hopes and strengths are determined to stay under cover and out of sight for the moment. There's something, something real to make you willing to mutter the basic, primitive, human confession, "I shouldn't be the way I am." If that can find honest voice in your heart, don't fail to hear God's answer to that one, "Well, you need not stay the way you are."

We're not talking about good resolutions here—this drawing up of a much-advertised contract with ourselves to shed all our faults like some cocoon, this blowing on our hands and flexing all our virtues for the acrobatics of chucking the whole catalogue of our discontents, with most of it a game, you know, tongue-in-cheek really, never meant to be much more than conversation pieces, since we might as well admit from that start we're always haunted by the suspicion that there's no way out of the ruts we're in! That whatever we are, we're stuck with ourselves as we are. That our days are grooved and patterned with all our tomorrows rather much the helpless pensioners of yesterday's errors, that this itch for self-improvement which breaks out among us like a seasonal rash isn't really worth the scratching, for there's no way out of the ruts we're in!

As a matter of fact, there isn't, if all our effort is on our own. But we're not on our own, not if that name *God* stands for something other than a hollow, monstrous mockery! Not if Jesus Christ is anything other than a genial, well-meaning fraud! Have you ever tried to face Him in your mind and think of Christ seriously as a fraud? We're not on our own. We don't make resolutions—we make vows. We don't blow on our hands—we bow our heads. There's many a ruined, wasted yesterday we pray to be cut free from, not by any cleverness of ours but by the shock of God's love!

It's then that we clench our fists. It's then we call to attention all our sleeping determination and tether our wills to that moment and pledge that in this or this or this, tomorrow will be better, so help us God! Half promise, half prayer! You say, "But it won't last." They always clubbed old Governor Campbell back into the gutter with that one. It won't last. *Of course it won't last! Who cares?* Who cares, if for a while it makes a real difference, if it can see you through until your heart can be caught again on the surge of another of God's incoming tides?

"That's the trouble with religion," they used to say, and

the barber would look up and listen as if to hear some final word on the matter. "You take old Governor Campbell—why, he gets converted at every revival." But all the while the tragedy was that he wasn't converted often enough. When will we see that difference between the way the village looks at a man and the way Christ sees him? With him there are no yesterdays. There's only today.

There are vows to be made to Him with every dawning. And if those vows are broken by evening, then thank God, He'll be there early next morning to help us pledge allegiance to Him all over again!

"We don't always say grace before meals at our house. But we take it for granted that God knows how grateful we are!"

—*The Hostess*

13

DOES GOD READ HIS CHILDREN'S MAIL?

DR. RALPH SOCKMAN insists that about once a year a preacher should bring to his people a message that's so odd, so off-beat, and so confusing that his people won't know what he's talking about, and this will re-establish his reputation among them as a deep thinker. When Dr. Sockman gives advice as to the care and feeding of congregations, it is not to be taken lightly, for this Prince of the American Pulpit has spent his entire remarkable ministry at one church in New York. Forty years! That's a jaw-gaping span, not only to be able to stand the same people, but to persuade the same people to stand him! And I suspect this advice of his as to the merit of an annual pulpit-puzzler applies only to him and the few like him, and not to the rest of us who can be confusing without even trying, fifty-two Sundays a year.

Yet, let me confess that Dr. Sockman's advice does occur to me whenever I brace myself to tackle this theme. Not as a motive, you'll understand, but bringing at least a faint, ten-watt glow of consolation and comfort. *Because what I want*

*to share with you now is bound to raise more questions than
it even attempts to answer.* It is bound to issue in a measure of
confusion because I'm puzzled about it from the start. But it
walks right up to you as something to be faced if we're to
make living sense of God's way with men.

Let's begin it with the familiar experience of what an embarrassment it is to be the hostess when a clergyman is present
at the dinner table and some member of her family begins to
eat before grace is said. There's always the quick reprimand,
and the shocked look on the face of the offender, and then the
clergyman offers grace in the strained silence, usually grateful
that this same family has never watched him trying to keep
his children back from the trough until after prayers. Then
all is well and quite understandable, unless the host or hostess
feels called upon to explain.

It's amazing how often the explanation will seem to follow
a prepared script. The hostess will say, "We don't always say
grace before meals at our house." This has been fairly obvious,
but the cornered clergyman butters his roll and waits because
he knows there's another line to this script. "But," she adds, and
this usually with a rallying smile and somewhat breezily said,
*"but we take it for granted that God knows how grateful we
are!"*

"We don't bother to thank God here at the table! Why should
we? He knows how grateful we are!" Well, that's reasonable.
That figures, according to the quick logic of the dinner table.
The trouble is it won't stay at the dinner table. It leaves the
table and roams all over the house. If God reads every thought
in our minds, then why pray at all? If He knows at every moment what we're thinking, why go through the motions of
telling Him what He already knows? Let Him go ahead and
read our minds. It's all there, plain to His eyes.

Or is it? Suddenly you remember that strange, remarkable twist of logic Christ once used when He spoke of prayer. "Don't make your prayers a harangue," He warned the disciples. "Don't go on and on in fulsome wordy repetitions as you've heard both the heathen and the hypocrite use. Remember that God your Father knows what you need before you ask Him."

Almost—almost what we said back at the dinner table, isn't it? Then surely Christ's conclusion too will be, "Don't bother to pray." But that is *not* His conclusion. Not on your life it isn't. What He says is, "Therefore, do pray!" God already knows what you need, therefore pray simply, honestly, earnestly.

What kind of a switch is that? You find it throughout the New Testament. You find it on every page of the long, rich story of Christian experience. Always, when faith is strong and vital there is on the one hand this vivid belief that there is at the core of life the Great Person watching you and me from the wings every moment that we're on stage, peering at us through the pasteboard scenery of life, the eyes of Him who knows us through and through. Yet that basic belief walks arm in arm with this other insistence that you must keep in touch with Him, that you must take pains to make your desires known unto Him, and keep opening your heart to Him.

How can you square the one with the other? It sends us back to that dinner table daring to ask a very queer question. Our hostess says, "We take it for granted God knows how grateful we are." *But what if He doesn't?* What if He doesn't know unless He's told or shown? What if that's one of the rules of God's game, that He will not eavesdrop at the keyhole of our souls unless there's some indication of welcome, that He will not slip in to read our minds unless some signal is given? What if, because of that magnificent sportsmanship by which the

Almighty has set up rules for Himself to go by, in the lifelong contest for our souls, *what if God refuses to read His children's mail unless it's addressed to Him?*

Let's use that homely analogy, because didn't Christ show us once and for all in the parables that it's by such warmly, awkwardly human comparisons that we catch a plainer glimpse of the truth than by all the heavy, labored logic of the sages? You and I have our opinions, and they are not high opinions, of parents who will not respect their maturing children's sacred right of individuality—parents who, because of a shameless curiosity, or a morbid possessiveness, or a hard emotional tyranny, will stoop to any guile to control their children, will even slip around and open their personal mail. We don't like that in ourselves. What if Almighty God is too much a gentleman for that sort of thing, too? What if He is too honourable a Father ever to steam open some sealed flap of our thinking, ever to take some thin envelope of our minds and hold it up against the light of His eternal vigilance? *What if God, even though He could, simply refuses to read our mail unless it's somehow addressed to Him?* Wouldn't that play hob with all our cheap and easy notions of what it means to be religious, of what religious living really is?

Your first reaction to that should be, "Why, this is heresy. You're shrinking God. You're putting a limit on the knowledge and power of God. You're saying there are some things He can't know and do. Don't we call Him the Almighty?"

Yes, that's what we call Him. And it's a shame we say it so glibly, without thinking what we're saying. That's exactly what faith means. He's Almighty. No one limits the power of God. But there are limits God has set for Himself.

The most amazing limitation He ever set for Himself was not when He meshed and grooved and balanced this incredible maze of energy in control which we call our universe and set it up as this vast timepiece, to tick away undisturbed till He is through with it. No, the most startling curb God ever put on His powers was when He made you and me, this mortal experiment, this hunting expedition. He arranged in time for something He had dreamed in eternity. He who could force anything, created something He refused to force: the human story, a plot awaiting the human decision, because of this flaw, this scandal in a law-abiding universe, human freedom. So far as we can tell and so far as we've been told, you are the only thing in the universe that can keep God at bay, holding Him off at arm's length forever.

C. S. Lewis has pictured the devil presiding at one of the councils of hell and instructing all the shades and shapes of evil as to what they're up against. "Remember," the devil warns in effect, "disgusting as it may seem to you, God really loves those weak and filthy human vermin that crawl the earth. Hateful as it may seem to you, He really wants them finally happy. That's why God did that treacherous thing we here in hell will never understand: cut them loose from His control, put human beings on their own in so many dangerous ways, took some of His own freedom and slipped it into their beastly little hearts. That's why He's so mysterious with them, and plays His awful game of hide-and-go-seek with them. He wants something more than mere obedience. *His master plan is to win from them the free unforced recognition of His love, and the free unforced and glad response to it!*"

Two thousand years of Christian thought have been able to peer at least that far into the mystery of why God's even in this business of living with you and me. And that's probably as far as we were meant to see. Surely, it is worth betting a life on! But now and then we'll surely be forgiven if we edge up to the limits of our knowledge and try at least a quick and tentative glance beyond them.

*What if one part of the package of freedom is the freedom
to communicate with God or not to?* What if the freedom to
beam our thoughts, hopes, desires and intentions in His direc-
tion or not to, so that He who knows our needs—knows us far
better than we'll ever know ourselves—could be cut off by us,
tuned out by us? Here in this tiny, built-in sending and receiv-
ing set of our minds, when we're so wrapped up in concerns
that have no room in them for God, so snarled up in devices
of heart that God can neither approve, direct, or bless, what if
that jams the circuits, breaks the contact—and for that hour,
that day, that month there registers on the Eternal Awareness
only the crackling buzz of a meaningless static where we're
concerned?

Then something of the constant heartache of God could be
phrased in household terms, with God saying, "Why, I haven't
heard from him for days. I haven't made contact with him for
days. I see what he's up to yonder, but how can I help? How
can I give him his bearings if he goes on refusing to get in
touch with me?"

Oh, we probably can't go further with it than the bare hint
as a figure of speech. But doesn't even the hint of it underscore
some old truth with a strange new urgency? How foolish all
our obvious little pro and con arguments about prayer would
be then, for prayer would be no mere luxury item for the lei-
surely heart, but the necessity, the basic thrust, the test pattern
for all our communications.

And what would be on God's wave-length, if you please—
what would He feel welcome to overhear, welcome to listen
in on even when not consciously invited? Why, surely all
honest search for truth, and surely all honestly-intentioned
thoughts of faith, and hope and love—surely these would get
through to Him no matter where they were aimed.

And Christ, of course—now think of that! Christ would even

be the video phase of our communication with God—not just truth heard or felt but seen, brought into focus whenever we actually summon Christ into our minds, all God's desire to get through to us and all our desire to get through to Him meeting and merging into Someone we recognize!

Does it make any kind of sense? Does it suggest anything? Say anything? If so, think on it, and may God lead you through it to some source of strengthened faith. If not, take comfort at least in this: you and I have been thinking about reality. Not shadows, but living reality, God and our souls, and thinking about them as if they were real, and not shadows. And even though our best thought will err, nothing but good can come of having spent some moments together sensing how real He is, and how hungry we are to know it!

"He's got the whole world in His hands.
He's got the wind and the rain in His hands,
He's got the sun and the moon right in His hands.

* * *

He's got the little bitsa baby in His hands,

* * *

He's got you and me, brother, in His hands,
He's got you and me, sister, in His hands.

* * *

Oh, He's got everybody in His hands,
He's got everybody here right in His hands,
He's got the whole world in His hands."

—*The Cocktail Party*

14

THE WHOLE WORLD IN HIS
HANDS

IT WAS ONE of those late afternoons along the south Jersey sea-shore when you could have watched a crimson cloud bank trying to sheathe the setting sun; a glorious, determined sun it had been this day, and it still seemed rather unlikely that all its blades could be scabbarded except by the flat horizon.

Or you could have been down the beach, a scant two blocks away. The sun had been hot enough so that in spite of the steady sea breeze the sand would still have been warm to your feet. But the sea was now plotting against the beach in the tireless, ageless pattern of the incoming tide—the advance of breakers rushing up to sprawl and foam across the sand with surprising lack of dignity, and then, with a playful show of hypocritical timidity, a quick retreat, as if the sea didn't know very well who would win. As if the beach didn't know the giant was only flexing its muscles to reach farther on the next try.

The surf would have been just right for the more deter-minedly athletic bathers, out there where the slow rollers politely waited their turn as if nodding to each other, "after you," and signaling their readiness by rearing for one moment to expose "the dark green sheen of their flanks" before they raced to spend themselves.

But the lifeguards had left their stations, those hulking, massive lifeguards burned to the color only lifeguards and lobsters seem ever to achieve. And the beaches were very nearly deserted. The people had streamed back to their cottages suddenly, like lemmings in reverse, as if an unheard signal had been given, hurrying along in the various stages of undress that would look so ridiculous anywhere else in the world but seemed absurd here only when it verged on the grotesque. They had hurried to their temporary homes, to hurry and change and hurry to something else, for they had to keep at it like dedicated beavers, this exhausting business of getting a rest.

So backs were turned, if many of them unwillingly, on that ocean, that somehow sacramental ocean, at the very time of day when it might have had the most to say to us one by one, at the very time of day when it might have washed fretful minds with its primitive therapy, erasing all yesterday's botchy little scribblings with today's clean tides that keep trying to remind the shore of power and patience and eternity. There it surged two blocks away, waiting for some heart to notice. There it preached along the beaches, but who was listening?

For across the street from us and down the block to the left, an astonishing number of people were crowding onto a wide front porch for a cocktail party that was to prove to be quite a party. It was a rambling, three-story, gray-shingled house of surprising size. All winter you knew it would look like a sinister abandoned hotel, the kind of place to which you might invite Alfred Hitchcock for a fortnight of inspiration. But here in the summer it came alive and bristled with occupants, and this particular evening not even the word "bristle" could do justice.

The deep, almost cavernous looking porch had been stripped of its furniture; even the wicker chairs, which had that sprung look as if they had been "frozen in the very act of collapsing," had been removed to make more room for the human traffic. And at the rate they were arriving you got the impression you were witnessing that rare nightmare of hostesses when absolutely everyone invited had decided to come, with no 30 per cent comfortable margin of regrets, every blessed one responding, "Why, Myrtle, we'd love to, darling, what time?"

They tended to be dressed in what for lack of a more exact phrase I'd call "Philadelphia informal—" every era represented from the fringe to the sack—dowagers as colorful as regatta boats, and men in shorts who knew they weren't the type, since so few are, so they had tried to atone for that lack of realism with a limp but uncomfortably proper blue coat. And two caterers, in their only slightly soiled white jackets, moved as well as they could move in and around the tightening squeeze of new arrivals, with set smiles and that long-suffering patience won by having catered ten thousand such parties.

And I sat across the street unashamedly wishing that I dared to get my field glasses and sit there like some bird watcher for a close-range observance of the care and feeding habits of a nestful of specimens. They were already beginning the larger-than-life voices and gestures that would grow louder and more exaggerated as this strange American ritual progressed, and the buffet table and the coffee urns set over in the corner went untouched.

Oh, please don't get it out of focus, now. Please remember what it seems so difficult for us ever honestly to get straight: the frightening clarity of Jesus Christ's insistence that if I, across the street, just sat there in the seat of the scornful, warming the hands of my own self-righteousness over the meager glow of my satisfied observance of some poor little punctilios of proper conduct, I would have been doing my soul a hundred times over more wrong than they necessarily were doing theirs.

The mood in which to watch them was one of amazement and concern that here were people, refugees from the crowds they wrestled with through the year, who needed so to rediscover how to be alone now and then. And vacation was their chance—but here they were ganging together on a porch, as closely packed as so many chips in a tuna can. Yet give the tuna credit: he has to be caught to be canned.

They needed so desperately some quiet from the noise and distractions they knew year-round, this bedlam of telephones and traffic, where newspapers wrap us in megaphones for broadcasters to shout through. But here they were, jammed cheek to jowl and screaming at each other, to be heard above the hi-fi that was going full blast.

They needed so some time out, some time off, to get acquainted with themselves as real people, to dig down under the clutter of all they kept pretending to be because of what others expected them to be—some hours when their hearts could go naked, if you please, drop the masks, the poses, the pretenses and disguises which we all wear to hide from the world. But here they were, hurrying to let their own small voices of individuality be drummed to a stupor by the herd.

Oh, I could go on as you could, as I did through our supper time and after, thinking what a picture it was of us all, there by the sea and the sand and the sunset. These who huddled together with their backs to all that, packing their loneliness and need into the loneliest place in this world, the crowd, the superficial crowd, the bluffing, tyrannical, frightened crowd.

I could have gone on because the party went on. As darkness fell, you could tell by the quickened tempo and crescendo of noise and strident laughter that it was on the verge of becoming a great success. The guests were beginning to sing. At first just a few with off-key but take-charge voices, then more of them and more until people up and down the block began to wander past on the sidewalk with undisguised curiosity, and you noticed the car of the local police chief driving slowly back and forth, as the inevitable choruses of "Harvest Moon" and "The Sweetheart of Sigma Chi" rang out with slur and blur and moist soprano and ululating tenor, but heartily and unmistakably.

And suddenly, I couldn't believe what I was hearing. Without warning, with the same near-hysterical gusto, do you know what they were singing? *"He's got the whole world in His hands. He's got the whole world in His hands."* Verse by verse and after each verse, laughter and applause. Laughter and applause! I don't know that I've ever before envied so the medieval gesture of making the sign of the cross to ward off something ominous and threatening.

Do you know that magnificent spiritual as Marian Anderson sings it? Not the raucous version of it they waxed last year for the rock 'n' roll set, but the way she sings it with all the awe and wonder and strength of trust and commitment with which it must be sung if it's to be an affirmation and not a mockery.

This the crowd was singing, verse by verse. "He's got the sun and the moon right in His hands"—then laughter. "He's got the wind and the rain in His hands"—then cheers. "He's got the little bitsa baby in His hands"—then loud applause. "He's got you and me, brother, in His hands"—then much clapping and roaring of approval.

And two blocks away, the timeless surf pounded on the beach. And the sea breeze blew clean and clear, and the eye of the moon winked open over the water. And I thought, along that borderline between oath and prayer, *Oh, God, if it's to this our vaunted return to religion has brought us, then this is the way the world ends, not with a bang, not even with a whimper, but with an off-key song and a sob!*

But isn't it true, what they were singing? Couldn't it be classified as praise "out of the mouths of babes," you know? Oh, it's true! He's got the whole world in His hands, the All-powerful, All-knowing, the Ever-present whom we call God. But it is not true the way they were singing it. It is not drunkenly true. It is not sloppily true. It is not sentimentally true. It is not easily and obviously and laughingly true. *This is no "Sweet Adeline" theology.* It is strangely and mysteriously and both wonderfully and terribly true. Somehow, Someone bigger than the universe has hold on the universe, for it's His doing and it does what He tells it, and we pygmies can't go against the grain of it without getting splinters.

Somehow, Someone bigger than nature has hold on the forces of nature, though here the plot thickens and you can't believe the play without some other acquaintance with the Author. For there's far more to nature than the surf and the beach and the sunset. There's also the baffling horror of the hurricane and the tidal wave. There's what stares at us from the cold beady eye of the cobra, and rustles with the tarantula and lurks in the death-bite of a virus so tiny we can't even see it. You can find a God in nature but if that's all you have to go on, about all you can talk about is His ingenuity and His sheer inscrutable power.

But Someone bigger than mankind has hold somehow on mankind too, and mankind is forever forgetting—or never quite learning—that that means either dawn or doom for any age, whichever it decides. His hold on our race is tight enough to accomplish what He wills and intends, but loose enough always to give humanity its choice: is it to be the instrument of what He plans, or the obstacle and the victim? Don't gloss over that, don't mislay that thought when you try to make some Christian sense of our tragic day: *earth's unhappiness comes never by God's intention, but with God's reluctant permission,* when we prove to be determined that that's the way we're going to have it.

But what about you? You and me? "You and me, brother, in His hands"?

Yes, He who has hold of the universe so magnificently, He who has hold of nature so strangely, He who has hold of man-kind so mysteriously, has hold of you. Not as a man clutches some toy possession, though you mean more to Him than a toy ever meant to a child or a gem to a miser. Not as a puppe-teer dangles a puppet, though He has ten thousand strings to pull on your heart, of which a puppeteer never dreamed.

He holds you as a better Father than the world has ever known would want to hold an only son. You're His, but you're free to act as if you are not. "Life is nearer to God than any-thing we can make out of life. Men are nearer to God than they ever are to each other. Each of us is nearer to God than to anyone else in the world." But you're free to run from that, forget it, deny it, act as if you want no part of it, or admit it but not mean it and do nothing about it.

He won't force you, not now, not for a while. Not while there's still the chance that somehow He can win from you the free, unforced decision, "I will arise and go to my Father." He'll wait for that. Each of us has a while. But none of us has as long as he thinks he has. That's why those people on that porch, those poor, silly, posing, lonely, frightened people on that porch were so very right in what they were singing—but in the way they were singing it, so terribly, tragically wrong.

"All his life he kept getting ready for something, kept looking forward to something. If there's any sense in it, if there's anything right about all of it, he has found what he was after."

—*The New Widow*

15

WHAT IT TAKES TO MAKE EASTER

IT WAS EASTER TIME. We sat in a room I disliked intensely, but the fault was mine rather than the room's. I happen to dislike any room that has been tidied up for sorrow, everything in its place, all arranged so orderly and unnaturally, as if some pattern of neatness in life's furniture can be some measure of refuge for a heart in shock. She was dressed for sorrow, in her best. That is another curious yet understandable habit of ours. We can be casual with gladness, it seems, but we have a determination to look our best when heartbreak tries to stare us down. Outside, it was almost spring, which is no guarantee that there won't be some more winter to follow, yet here and there is a day such as that one, quick as a slap or a kiss to remind you how spring will feel when it does come gently and for good.

She sat quietly, the only evidence of her intensity the tilt of her chin and the way she slowly twisted the ring on her finger. She was at that age where the girl that she had been still looked out at me through the face of the woman she was.

133

When she spoke, the words were not aimed at me, though I knew I was welcome to eavesdrop; she said it to herself as if to strike some working balance between her hopes and her doubts; she said it to God as if God should be ashamed if it were not true: *"All his life he kept getting ready for something, kept looking forward to something. If there's any sense in it, if there's anything right about all of it, he has found what he was after."*

That may not strike you as the most ringing, convinced, contagious declaration of faith, but it went through me like high voltage, because I know that young widow was not speaking as a thoroughly convinced Christian; she was speaking as a thoroughly cornered human being. And if you could take Easter out of the world, if you could by some terrible erasure brainwash Easter from mankind's memory and experience, just sponge it off the record, what that woman said would be the best we would have. Without planning it or rehearsing it, she had summed up what the human race in the main and at its best has found itself determined to believe. It doesn't seem to matter where you find us, in what land or time; it may be some stone-age man staring puzzled out of his lonely cave at an evening sky, some noble of Egypt's Middle Kingdom planning his family tomb, some nameless and forgotten slave condemned for life to the mines of Carthage carving crude but powerful symbols on the walls of his dark tunnels, or magnificently ugly old Socrates consoling those young gods who stood around him as the hemlock began to take its effect, or strange John Brown trundling along in an army wagon the morning of his execution saying of that Virginia countryside, "This is a beautiful country; I'd really never noticed it before," or a lad trekking down a battered trail in Korea and someone asking, "What stopped Jamie?" and his answering through a grim clench of teeth, "Nothing stopped

Jamie"—"But he got it, didn't he?" "Yeah, he got it, whatever it is, but nothing will ever stop him; Jamie is not expendable!" It all gives our secret away, if you'll watch it carefully, from Crete to Texas; even though we may choose to spend our years as if it could not possibly be true, even though we may deliberately force and train our minds to argue cleverly that it cannot possibly make sense, still we have a deep, hidden secret, and *that secret is that you and I came equipped with a built-in inclination to expect life to have some kind of sequel beyond death.*

From a complex of reasons, Mark Twain's laughter dried up in his later years; he grew terribly cynical and bitter, with nothing but satire and invective for any creed. Yet he said to friends this revealing thing: "I can't understand it; I've successfully exploded every possible argument for an after-life, and in spite of that I fully expect there to be one!" He had overlooked the fact that he was built that way. The strange blueprint according to which you and I were assembled has so put us together that along with everything else that rattles around in the confusion of these narrow clay closets there's something within us knows we were shaped to fit beyond a grave, and those who have been honest enough with themselves and with life to admit this often embarrassing secret have called it a good many things—"the instinct for immortality," "the soul's invincible surmise," "the deathless hope no man can quite escape." Some under the bite of grief say it as simply and as defiantly as that young widow did. Some say it with passion and poetry, as Thomas Wolfe poured it out: "The minute-winning days, like flies, buzz home to death." But we, he said, you and I, "We seek the great forgotten language, the lost lane-end into heaven, a stone, a leaf, an unfound door." It is one of the by no means minor miracles of Easter that it is a day when we feel it is permissible for this shy, em-

barrassed instinct of ours to come out of hiding and let itself
be looked over to re-assess what more than this it takes really
to make it Easter.

Don't misunderstand me; I'm not even pretending that you
would find widespread conscious agreement among us as to
exactly what we believe about this. That's part of the strange
excitement of Easter worship—not just that so many of us come
to church, but *that so many of us come to church who couldn't
really tell why we come. How many are there who have made
up their minds that this is a matter on which you can't make
up your mind*—that if anything lies on the other side of death
it will take care of itself in time—meanwhile, the less said
about it the better? Like Robert Frost, you'll "wait and see"?
Well, to you Easter says, "Be very careful of that pose of non-
chalance, that typically modern attempt to postpone even thinking about it. Your heart knows better than that. Your heart
knows that until you in some way make up your mind about
that other life, you can't even make up your mind about *this*
life, and you certainly can't make up your mind about the
goodness and love and power and wisdom of God!"

*How many are there who have been caught in the trap of
days so difficult* you're not certain at the moment that this
business of another chapter, another installment is so attractive after all? You're so tired of being yourself at the moment
that the thought of being yourself forever disturbs rather than
comforts you; you're ready to quote Swinburne's words when
he thanked,

> . . . with brief thanksgiving
> Whatever gods may be,
> That no life lives forever,
> That dead men rise up never;
> That even the weariest river
> Winds somewhere safe to sea.

Well, to *you* Easter says, "That is your weariness that's talking, and not you at your best. When we are weak we feel like that; there are times when our mood is that we couldn't care less! It's in hours of strength, when the tide of life runs high in us again, when our love for others insists on the deathless value of people we have known, when possibilities open up within us too fine and deep and meaningful for any short lifetime to wear them out—it's when we're at our best that this ageless demand in our hearts to have the chance of going on makes sense."

And certainly, in a modern church, we have to ask, "*How many are there who are still so resentful of the nursery rhyme religion of your childhood,* the crude cartoons of eternity, the know-it-alls who could tell you so exactly about the furniture of heaven and the temperature of hell that you've a mental block on the subject?" You'd agree with Dean Inge that the only thing worse than the old notion of singing anthems eternally would be to be condemned to listening to anthems eternally; you just can't imagine what a future life could be. Well, to you Easter says, "Good for you—so far as it goes! Just don't let it stop at that." Of course, here in time, we try to imagine a life beyond time; of course, when we whose every thought is colored by our temporary dependence on these bodies try to imagine an existence independent on these bodies, our pictures of eternity are liable to be no closer to the facts than a child's house of blocks is like the Taj Mahal. But all that means is that our best imagination of the soul's adventure, when it steps free, gets through, "To lose the earth you know, for greater knowing; to lose the life you have, for greater life; to leave the friends you loved, for greater loving; to find a land more kind than home, more large than earth—" Our best imagination of what that will be like will prove to be but little paper-match flares in the blinding light of Reality!

But someone says, "You're giving us no arguments." And you'll be right. For arguments there are, but let's wrangle over them some other day, any other day. *Easter is no time for argument.* Lilies don't argue; they bloom. Springtime doesn't argue; it comes. Music doesn't argue; it sings. Beauty doesn't argue; it beckons and points. Love doesn't argue; it just outlives our griefs. *This is Easter* if we'll let it be a day for remembering what the world will bluff and bribe and bully us out of whenever it can—the remembering of how much is at stake in our daring to believe this that we shyly want to believe. It isn't just a matter of our personal cry for some kind of survival. The whole demand of our minds, that this life we're involved in make some final sense and add up to something worth adding, is at stake here. Every thrust our conscience ever gave to the word "justice" is at stake here. Every promise life has ever made to us through someone we honestly love is at stake here. Everything that has ever been worth saying about God is at stake here. Let Easter be a day of hearing again, that the only person who ever fully lived the eternal life right before our eyes, the life of that other world here in this world, could not be stopped by death. It could not close Him out of either world. He came back. He came back to some people who, God knows, were not expecting Him to come back. They were broken-hearted, disillusioned, bewildered and despairing people, but suddenly they were blazingly reassured, for suddenly dawn came, suddenly the stone was no barrier, the unfound door was open wide enough and long enough to see Him there. He said to Mary, "Don't try to detain Me; hurry and tell the others, especially Peter." He said to Thomas, "You wanted to see my hands and this scar on my side." When He met the two on the road to Emmaus he actually laughed at their gloom and asked them, "Why are you so slow of heart to believe?"

This is Easter if you can answer "yes" to these questions:

"Will you try again to live as if this were true in a world that has driven itself nearly mad from doubting it? Will you act if this were not just some hope to die by but a glad creed to live by? Will you keep coming back through every mystery and doubt, through all unanswered questions, through every disappointment and seemingly needless sorrow? Will you keep coming back to this faith that Christ signed God's own autograph across the deepest yearnings of your heart, and that what we care for most is not finally at the mercy of what we care for least? In view of that will you try to live as if you knew that one way or the other, you're never really going to die?"

Of course, you'll have to have Christ's help to say "yes" to that. But He's what it takes to make Easter.

"When everything else has been solved, coming back to earth may prove to be our toughest problem."

—*The Space Engineer*

16

ON COMING BACK TO EARTH

I'VE BEEN OBTUSE and slow, lately, to realize what has been in back of several conversations I've been drawn into with several people of no particular faith who do not know me except to know that I am a clergyman. They have brought up the subjects which have a good part of the world flap-mouthed and fish-eyed at the moment: the headlines announcing the dawning of the era of interplanetary travel, the sober probability that man may well within this decade rocket himself into the endless emptiness of outer space, even the cautiously admitted possibility by some heretofore conservative scientific oracles that there may be life comparable to ours somewhere else in this universe.

I've been mystified as to why these people have talked to me the way they have about all this, not in search of information heaven knows—they consider themselves quite adequately informed—but in a peculiar, off-the-cuff, almost conspiratorial attitude of "Now forget that you're a minister for a moment, and tell us what you really believe about all this. We won't tell on you!" Slowly, it has dawned on me, "Why, bless their little hearts, not to mention their little heads, *they honestly think*

141

*that as a clergyman I'm not officially allowed to be receptive to
such revolutionary views of technological advance and human
potential.* They haven't any but the scrappiest, rag-tag notion
of what that Biblical point of view is, but they assume the
Space Age is somehow an embarrassment to the Bible! They
assume it's still the first order of business for us in the church
to be carrying on the six-hundred-year-old petty warfare between religion and science, that we're still arguing with Dar-
win and not even too happy about Galileo, that for us the
Scopes trial is still before the jury and we're still sharpening
arguments with which the white knight William Jennings
Bryan can slay the dragon Clarence Darrow.

I find myself at a loss as to what to say to such people
to bring them up to date. You tell them that every true advance
science has ever made in showing us a vaster universe has
simply stretched our realization of how vast a God this is we
worship, and they just look at you suspiciously. You mention
that, viewed in a number of ways, atomic fission simply serves
as a terrifying footnote to half the texts of the Bible, and they
glance uneasily at one another. You suggest that the official
reaction of the Christian Church, should we ever discover life
on Mars, would possibly be to feel a little sorry for the planet
Mars. Why, the Martians may be doing all right up there without us! Imagine transplanting some of the people you know to
a possibly innocent and unsuspecting civilization! Oh, you
may find the thought attractive, you may have some ready
suggestions, but it would hardly be a bargain for Mars. We
sons and daughters of Adam and Eve have enough trouble
up our sleeves to infect the entire solar system.

By the time you've said all that, these space-age conversa-
tionalists will be trying desperately to change the subject;
they'll have written you off as not only an odd stick, but very
unorthodox religiously. But like any compulsive conversation-

alist, that is when I don't want the subject changed. It's right
there I want to give, as source material for their future stalking
and baiting of unsuspecting preachers, my own confessions of
a not-entirely-reformed reader of science fiction.

I knew more about space-travel twenty-five years ago than
I'll ever know again—much to my poor mother's despair.
She thought of these fantastic yarns about the time stream,
and the fourth dimension, and colonies on the moon and the
Martian canals, and the conquest of the planets, with the same
disapproval with which she'd have viewed French novels!
How it would upset her to catch me in my earliest teens curled
up by the hour with a paper-bound volume of science fiction
slipped cunningly inside some approved volume of the Rover
Boy series or the latest Tom Swift! Perhaps it would have
been better for me to have been out on the playground—but
the teens are the teens, and as a recipe for getting out of this
world I'll still prefer H. G. Wells to rock 'n' roll!

But mother was determined to take steps to save me from
the sorceries of such unsound fantasy, and her trump card was
to hail me at last before our minister, our beloved Dr. Todd. A
massive, acrobatic bear of a man, as well-equipped mentally
as he was full-cushioned physically, he held our community
in the strong grip of his heart and hands with room to spare.
I can remember writhing in an agony of knuckle-cracking
embarrassment as she reported her distress at my reading
aberrations, but I was quick to notice his reaction seemed to
be a scarcely-controllable amusement. He announced he
would let us both in on a secret. He led us into his inner
study and showed his collection of—yes, science fiction. Shelf
upon shelf of it, titles I had never heard of, he had them all.
My mother couldn't have been more shocked if he had showed
us a secret wine cellar. I'm not certain she ever completely
regained her total trust in clergymen. But I was allowed to

bring my science fiction out of hiding from under the bed and to display it unashamed right there in the company of Kipling and London and Mark Twain.

I thought in all fairness you should have some such confession from a misspent youth to explain the point of view with which a would-be Christian could stand beside a newsstand this week, looking at the headlines, leafing through the journals, noticing the features (space suits, space ships, hard facts and prophecies! The eerie perils to be overcome! Even the time table for an ion engine! To Mars in one year, to Saturn in two years, to Jupiter in one and one-half years!) and take it all in not with any sense of amazement or astonishment but quite as a matter of fact, even with a kindling sense of recognition and familiarity in seeing about to come to pass things long since described and dreamed, with the only question, "Why has it been so long delayed?"

Every now and then I am told by some provincial pseudo-intellectual who has never worn the spurs of either science or religion, who would be as much at a loss with a test tube as he is with the Ten Commandments, that this dawning latest, potentially greatest technological advance by mankind is somehow in the nature of an embarrassment to the Christian faith! In the name of God, how is it an embarrassment? Why an embarrassment? What page of the Bible will it indict? What doctrine will it amend? What creed will it deny? Won't it rather reissue some Psalms, and reprint in capital letters such words as *"The heavens declare the glory of God; and the firmament sheweth his handywork"*? Won't it rather chant to those with ears to hear the swelling diapason of the praise, *"When I consider thy heavens, the work of thy fingers, the moon and the stars, which thou hast ordained; what an amazing piece of work is this pygmy man of whom thou hast been so mindful as to dare to create him a little lower than the angels and entrust him with such power"?*

Christians, if ever in our lives we took pride in, validly gloried in the wisdom of the Christian religion, let's take pride in it now! For in Christ alone lies the sanity that can keep you and me from those two fatal extremes: from hysterical, paralyzing fear of the doom and destruction a space age could bring upon us, and the equally hysterical hopes of some great new salvation to which the planets invite us. In all the spate of comment and opinion that has poured from those who know about these things, I've cherished most the possibly unconscious wisdom of the space engineer who said, *"When everything else has been solved, coming back to earth may prove to be our toughest problem.* The pioneers of the universe will still be in danger of a very prosaic and old-fashioned crash-landing."

Yes, very prosaic and old-fashioned, to be sure! This business of coming back to earth *will* be our constant problem. It can grow increasingly difficult for the citizen of a space age to remember that the most important bit of space in all the universe, so far as his responsibility is concerned, is the ground he's standing on now. Listen, not to a preacher, but to words from the columns of *The New York Times*: "The creature who descended from a tree or crawled out of a cave is now on the eve of incredible journeys. Yet it is not these journeys which chiefly matter. Will we be happier, wiser or better for seeing the other side of the moon or strolling in the meadows of Mars? The greatest adventure of all is not to explore the rings of Saturn. It is rather to try to understand the heart and the soul of man, to adventure in turning away from wrath and destruction toward creativeness and love." That was in *The Times*, but the accents are Christ's.

We'll get up there. Someone will. Perhaps some day soon.

And that will be tremendous news. The headlines will be a
foot high. We'll talk or think about little else for a while, until
we begin to realize that nothing has been found up there
that has changed the ground rules down here, that nothing has
been gleaned along the Milky Way which has made the good
life easier or the wrong less attractive. There is nothing out
there that can warm one heart chilled with loneliness here, or
bandage one mind that's been bleeding to death from doubt,
or forgive one sin that has turned one soul prematurely gray.
We may outwit the laws of gravity, but that will not teach us
any new way to outmaneuver the permanent emergencies of
the life you and I must live a day at a time, where forces
we never quite understand keep plotting and scheming the
defeat of our strength, the betrayal of our loves, the frustration
of our purposes, the question mark of innocent pain and the
exclamation point of death. No marvel that's to be scanned or
photographed or viewed out there can possibly compete with
the marvel of faith's insistence that the place where you're
standing *now* is holy ground; that the chance you have to become a child of God, God Himself is as concerned with as if
it were the only thing of consequence that's going on in all
the universe; that there will be no incredible journey embarked
on by the astronauts that finally will be seen to have compared
with the journey of your life in company with One who *was*
before the stars first shone, but who knows you by name,
One to whom the galaxies are tiny sets for the rings on His
fingers, but whose face is strangely familiar, and whose voice
is Galilean.

Long after all the stars are gone, He will still be there, and
one way or another, you'll still be there too.

"What if the world does end tomorrow, since there's nothing I can do about it? I don't even want to think about it. I've a date to play croquet with my aunt at two o'clock, for croquet is at least one thing I understand."

—*The Croquet Player*

17

WHAT CHRIST BELIEVES
ABOUT YOU

I WAS CONFRONTED recently by the challenge of a noted astronomer, brilliant in his own field, who was declaiming in the grand manner, "How dare you of the Christian Church have the effrontery to tell me, a trained, educated modern, that a young untaught Rabbi who lived over sixty generations ago and spent all His days in an underprivileged, postage-stamp country peopled by nonentities considered ignorant even in that barbaric day—how dare you tell me that He could know more about life than I do?"

Of course, when I heard that, I found myself bristling like an up-ended porcupine, thinking up all sorts of devastating replies—you know, the scorchers you never can think of at the moment but always think of later! Then I cooled down, telling myself that this was silly of me. *Why should I expect a man who has no particular knowledge of nor belief in nor feeling for Christ to make much sense when he talks about Christ?* Let that man lecture on astronomy. There are so many things he could help you and me to understand about astronomy. But it will take Jesus Christ to help me understand that lippy, cocky astronomer himself, as a man, as a needy human being in peril of his very soul, as potentially a child of God.

For Jesus knew what was in man. A sage of our day says, "It is strange that we mention so seldom the intelligence of Christ. We seem to notice everything else about Him except the fact that here was History's Supreme Genius of Common Sense, here was One who knew more about people than anyone has before or since." For Christians, that should be not an invitation to argument but to amazement. If He knew us that well, understood us that thoroughly, *how could He have had such high hopes for us, such expectations of us, as He does?* This Jesus was no mere naïve optimist. It is still a minor classic by the way of definitions that "a pessimist is simply some poor soul who has had to live ten years with an optimist." But the Galilean, far from looking only on the bright side of things, saw clearly our worst and still expected the best.

I know a man who greatly enjoys saying, "I'm very fond of the human race. All my family have belonged to it and even some of my wife's family too!" Compare the soft mockery of that with the way Christ could also say, "I am very fond of the human race," and punctuate it with pain and sign it not with ink but blood! What did He see in us that intrigued Him so? What did He find in you and me that would never quite allow an eclipse of His hope and admiration? Against the hours we spend in worship asking what do you believe about Christ, let's put a minute noticing some things Christ believes about you.

Christ believes that in so many of the things that really matter, you so often already know what is right, that what you need is the power to act on what you already know is true. Press the wine from the whole vintage of His teaching and it's remarkable in how much of it Jesus is the Great Reminder.

How often what He is doing is not so much announcing something new, but by some unforgettable figure of speech, some haunting story, some unavoidably clear picture He is reminding us of truths we already dimly sense but keep trying to evade and ignore and forget and avoid.

As Dr. Pitt Van Dusen has suggested, they came at Him with every kind of question about politics, religion, behavior. What should you do about a tyrant such as Caesar? How should you punish a woman who has been flagrantly immoral? Who's to be blamed for inherited diseases? What will be the marriage relationship in heaven? Sharp, tricky, loaded questions. Sometimes He came back with sharp, direct answers to clear the decks of nonsense with His breathtaking, "You've heard it said in former times, but I say unto you. . . ." Far oftener, He would come back at them with a counter-question, or a parable that tossed the question back to them, as much as to say, "Why would you ask such a thing of Me when you already know the answer, when any honest child knows the answer? Read it off your own heart in the light God has given you; stop deceiving yourselves that you're so ignorant about life; face up to the wisdom you already know but which is so comfortable for you to neglect or distrust or deny."

There have been many critics of Christianity, you know, across the years who have delighted in pointing to parts of the gospel and saying, "Why, this is old stuff! The prophets and the rabbis had already said that, Confucius had already taught that, Plato had said that!" How Christ would smile at such an objection. How patiently He would repeat His ageless answer, "Of course. I came not to destroy the best that mankind has known to be true. I came to fulfill it."

Christ believes that often, very often, when you and I clamor for new answers to our own problems, that we already know the answers. That's why one of our chief purposes in Christian worship is to be reminded of what we already know, to strike again vibrant notes which Christ has already hidden deep in the recesses of our hearts.

I feel sorry, to a degree, for you patient laymen who hear preachers year after year saying much the same things, because in any ten years you'll hear several versions of just about everything any one spokesman for religion has to offer you. But I can muster little more than impatience for that woman who complained to me bitterly about her clergyman who talked to her in a time of sorrow; she said, "He had nothing new to tell me to help me, just the same old business about Christ, the Resurrection and the Life, nothing different, just the same old thing." God help us, may she lose some of her taste for novelty before she comes to face the same old thing.

Because, you see, Christ also believes there are so very many answers you and I don't know, and for the time being aren't going to know. There's a galling, chafing irony to the tunester's phrase, "Ah, sweet mystery of life!" John Ruskin cried out on the kind of a day we all recognize, "I get so sick of the mysteries and puzzles, so tired of the hour by hour asking, 'Well, what can be made of this?' or 'Why did it come my way?' or 'What will come of it in time?'"

How long have you been climbing up the ladder of the uninvited hours from strange dawn to stranger dark, through turns and twists and some struggles you want no one to see, and others you wish to God someone would notice? As Samuel H. Miller has suggested, you hunt and fail and hope and now and then hide your pain, and keep trying with blundering hands to bless someone or something, and always and everywhere you're a little baffled by the desolate barren spaces mixed in with your hours of glory that almost hurt with happiness, the thrill of your incommensurable dreams, yet the tragic cost of your carelessness!

Where in this tenement of brittle bone and frail flesh, windowed by the senses, which people call *you,* where is the real *you?* What happens to this troubled handful of dust, breathing and snarling and scheming, that we should wrinkle our little brows and ponder on things eternal and claim to feel within ourselves something immortal? How have we dared, we earth animals, to call out across the timeless, windswept beaches of the universe our puny little challenge, "Who goes there?" and expect a Voice like our voice to answer, "God!"

Where can you find any foothold of sure understanding anywhere, especially today, in the baffling complexity of the sights and sounds and touch of this world of ours, this intricate, overpowering, unmanageable civilization that we thought was to be man's pride but now threatens to be man's death? So we're afraid! *Do you realize how much of the time we spend today running scared among silly amusements and slippery morals to keep from facing how frightened we are?* We're even afraid of too much joy; even our laughter is uncertain, even our affections hesitate. We open our hands but our hearts are covered, and we fear failure more than we love life, so we avoid the great ventures. As the man said in *The Croquet Player,* "What if the world does end tomorrow, since there's nothing I can do about it? I don't even want to think about it. I've a date to play croquet with my aunt at two o'clock, for croquet is at least one thing I understand."

There is a Man from Nazareth who sympathizes with our bewilderments. He always has. It's striking how gentle He always was with us about the real limits of our knowledge and the feebleness of our faith and our anxious, flickering zest for life. He has every respect for the mysteries before which we cower. But Christ does not believe that the Unknown, even for us, is absolutely Unknowable. He does not believe that the beating heart of Reality is even for us unintelligible. So what He did, says Dr. Nathan M. Pusey, president of Harvard, was this: *"In the depth of every mystery, Jesus put a Face!"* In the depth of every mystery He put a Face!

You see, Christ believes that you can make sense even of today's massive complexities, if you'll see them through the lens of certain tremendous simplicities! What or Who is behind this whirling madman's puzzle of darks and lights? Answer "God," and where will that get you? What do you mean by God, and what's He like? Can He possibly have any plans for, concerns with, attention to *us?* Fill the libraries with your definitions or your denials of God, spend the centuries arguing about Him, and still you will cry into the vastness, "Who goes there?"

Jesus says, "Your Father who is in heaven," and "If you've seen Me, you know what kind of a Father He is."

But what does He expect of us? We've heard ten thousand rules and each of those a thousand times denied. Even the rules we believe in we can't seem to keep, and even the good we know we can't quite seem to do. Jesus says "Follow Me. Cultivate My friendship as Someone whose company you want, and see how the rules take care of themselves."

But what is finally to come of it all? We've wracked our brains since man began to see some finale that can justify the struggle, to reason how this life we clutch so tightly, so briefly, could have some to-be-continued, and our wisest minds cannot reason it, and our most gifted tongues cannot express it. And Jesus says, "In My Father's House are many mansions. So much room. So much room. And you are so welcome."

There's a Man from Nazareth who believes no matter when the hour, you can take its measure through His eyes. Yes, you. He knows you. He knows all about you!